- Good Magazine 36
- Team engagement
  w/ brand + customers
    - staff video
    - p+/HCP video
    - FOC
    - YouTube content/page
    - Facebook
- Current CKD pt - social
  network?

More Praise for *The Dragonfly Effect*

"There's theory and there's applied theory. *The Dragonfly Effect* brings us all the way from the science into the execution. To me, it's that last mile that most of us miss. With this, you can take your ideas all the way through the last mile."

—Chris Brogan, author, *Trust Agents* and *Social Media 101*

"This truly innovative book identifies four powerful forces shaping our lives and shows how they are working together in unanticipated and creative ways. *The Dragonfly Effect* is fundamentally relevant to all younger leaders, who will spend their lives learning to leverage these forces, and to any leader from the baby boomer generation who wants to stay current with the role of social technology in business and our lives."

—Bill Meehan, director emeritus, McKinsey and Co., Inc.

"Too few executives take happiness seriously as a brand attribute, missing opportunities to build into products and services those features that would increase the overall delight and well-being of users and employees alike. Aaker and Smith have created an interesting, thoughtful, and engaging book to provoke new thinking about the power of joy."

—Joel Peterson, chairman, JetBlue Airways

"The Internet has made it possible for individuals and small groups to have an impact far beyond their size. Read *The Dragonfly Effect* to learn how to translate your good intentions into actual, real, tangible, world-changing good!"

—Avinash Kaushik, analytics evangelist, Google; and author, *Web Analytics 2.0*

"*The Dragonfly Effect* is an inspiration and a joy to read. Drawing on design thinking principles and emotional contagion, this is an important read for anyone contemplating the virality of ideas and creating infectious action. You will love it. It will transform you and your work."

—Pat Christen, president and CEO, HopeLab

"Motivating and inspiring, *The Dragonfly Effect* makes readers answer the question, 'how can I make an impact in the world?' with yet another question, 'what am I waiting for?' Aaker and Smith show you, whether acting as an individual or a corporation, how to harness the power of social media as a force for good, in a way that even a CFO will love."

—Lisa Edwards, head of Global Business Development, Visa Inc.

"This book takes the fast-evolving world of social media and offers a clear, inspiring guide to create social change."
—Bobbi Silten, CFO, Gap Inc.

"Aaker and Smith share rousing stories and a clear, powerful approach to using social media to produce positive impact. Creative minds will feel inspired and empowered."
—Chris Flink, associate professor, Hasso Plattner Institute of Design at Stanford

"Refreshing and compelling, *The Dragonfly Effect* provides a game plan to leverage social media for social good and bottom-line success. The need to efficiently and effectively connect with consumers is unchanging, but the means to do so is evolving quickly. Aaker and Smith show how to be truly connected at a deep, meaningful level."
—Jeff Weedman, vice-president for Global Business Development, Procter & Gamble

"If a dragonfly flaps its wings in Facebook, will it cause a social tsunami in Twitter? This book shows you how to align social actions to cause meaningful change. And that's what really matters in the era of new media."
—Brian Solis, principal, FutureWorks; and author, *Engage*

"Aaker and Smith created a beautifully visual book that's visionary yet practical. It proves that anyone can change the world."
—Nancy Duarte, CEO, Duarte Design; and author, *Slide:ology*

"An excellent read. *The Dragonfly Effect* offers a guidepost for every marketer struggling to stay on top of fast-evolving social media trends and use peer-to-peer marketing to mobilize a mass audience. Even more powerfully, the book demonstrates that by using our networks for good, we will be happier and more successful individuals—in life and at work."
—Joanna Drake Earl, COO, Current Media

"If you are ready to change the world, *The Dragonfly Effect* has the social networking secrets you've been looking for."
—Gregory Baldwin, president, VolunteerMatch

"*The Dragonfly Effect* is not only intelligent about social networks and getting action, but also has enormous amounts of research on persuasion, viral marketing, stickiness, and framing messages. Well-written and interesting, it should be a standard marketing text, and will be a wonderful reference for years to come."
—Jeffrey Pfeffer, author, *The Knowing-Doing Gap*

THE DRAGONFLY EFFECT

QUICK, EFFECTIVE, AND POWERFUL WAYS TO USE SOCIAL MEDIA TO DRIVE SOCIAL CHANGE

JENNIFER AAKER
ANDY SMITH
WITH CARLYE ADLER

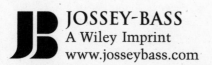

JOSSEY-BASS
A Wiley Imprint
www.josseybass.com

Published by Jossey-Bass
A Wiley Imprint
989 Market Street, San Francisco, CA 94103-1741—www.josseybass.com

Jossey-Bass books and products are available through most bookstores. To contact Jossey-Bass directly call our Customer Care Department within the U.S. at 800-956-7739, outside the U.S. at 317-572-3986, or fax 317-572-4002.

Jossey-Bass also publishes its books in a variety of electronic formats. Some content that appears in print may not be available in electronic books.

Library of Congress Cataloging-in-Publication Data

Aaker, Jennifer Lynn.
  The dragonfly effect : quick, effective, and powerful ways to use social media to drive social change / Jennifer Aaker and Andy Smith ; with Carlye Adler.
      p. cm.
  Includes index.
  ISBN 978-0-470-61415-0 (hardback)
  1. Internet marketing—Political aspects. 2. Social media—Political aspects. 3. Internet—Social aspects. 4. Social entrepreneurship. 5. Social responsibility of business. 6. Social change. I. Smith, Andy, 1968- II. Adler, Carlye. III. Title.
  HF5415.1265.A25 2010
  658.8'72—dc22

                                                      2010024706

Printed in the United States of America
FIRST EDITION
HB Printing   10 9 8 7 6 5 4 3 2 1

*Dedicated to Sameer Bhatia and to our children—
four wings of the dragonfly—Mia Adler Fieldman (Focus),
Cooper Smith (Grab Attention), Devon Smith (Engage),
and Téa Sloane Smith (Take Action)*

Contents

Foreword

Chip Heath, author of
Made to Stick and *Switch*

Everybody feels tremendous pressure today to master social media, but most people haven't quite figured out how to do so. Nonprofit directors are told they need a social media strategy for engaging volunteers. Journalists are encouraged to blog, tweet, and whirl. Marketers feel they're required to have a Facebook strategy. That's unfair to the poor marketers—heck, Facebook doesn't really have a Facebook strategy.

People who face serious problems have a long history of grasping for a technological fix. The 8-millimeter film was going to revitalize education . . . then the IBM PC. The Internet was going to usher in an era of political transparency. And for sure, positively, the magazine industry is going to be saved by the iPad. And today everyone feels that social media tools are a solution to the problems they are facing. (Except for those who are worried that someone else will figure out how to use them first and gain an enduring competitive advantage.)

So suppose you really could do something with social media. Well, *The Dragonfly Effect* points the way.

Full disclosure: Jennifer Aaker is one of my colleagues at Stanford. Her office is two doors down. I respect her research work, and I know this book is based on a class that has won rave reviews from our students. So I'm predisposed to like this book because I know it's based on serious research, ideas, and thought. (I don't really know her husband and coauthor,

Andy, but I suspect I'd like him too. I predict that one pressing question Jennifer and Andy will face when they speak about this book is, "How did you manage to write a book with your spouse?" Perhaps for their next project they'll consider a marriage guide.)

Disclosures noted, I think you'll like this book for the same reason our Stanford MBAs have loved Jennifer's class. In a confusing domain, where people haven't yet figured out how to use a new technology, Jennifer and Andy provide a simple road map to follow if you want to *accomplish* something with social media.

The book is filled with inspiring stories. A group of friends who rallied to save the life of a friend who had leukemia, and turned a one-in-twenty-thousand chance of finding a bone marrow donor into a virtual certainty. Two students who created a fashion business for an audience that hates fashion—guys— and managed to break even their first year and profit the second. The former nightclub promoter who, by telling riveting stories, created a movement that's brought clean water to eight hundred thousand people. And more important, there's a simple framework that highlights what these success stories have in common.

If you want to accomplish something with social media, you can start here. Just turn the page.

Preface

S mall actions create big change. The goal of this book is simple: to help you harness social technology to achieve a single, focused, concrete goal.

In the past ten years, social networking technologies have revolutionized the way we communicate and collaborate online. Each day, over 175 million of us log on to Facebook. Each minute, twenty hours of video are uploaded to YouTube. Each second, over 600 tweets are "tweeted" out onto the Web, to a worldwide audience. And these numbers are growing exponentially.

If we used these avenues for social change, what kind of difference could we make? How many people could we get involved? What kind of impact could we have on an individual, a corporation—or the world? Our mission over the following pages is to show you how to harness the power of social media for social good, by blending the theory underlying social change and the applications of social media. Our approach, which we call the *Dragonfly Effect*, coalesces the focal points of our distinct careers—research and insights on consumer psychology and happiness (what *really* makes people happy as opposed to what they *think* makes them happy)—with the practical approaches necessary to capture these effects.

Over the past several years, we have each benefited from the other's very different perspective. (Let's just say one of us didn't "get" Twitter and the other doubted the place of "feelings" in organizations.) By joining forces, we have been able to provide individuals and corporations with insights into social technology, tools to spur the spreading of ideas, and the ability to incite infectious action. Our capacity to predict seemingly irrational responses has improved both brands and bottom lines.

Most recently, our blended perspectives culminated in a course, the Power of Social Technology (PoST), at the Stanford Graduate School of Business. In the class, students adopted design thinking mind-sets and creative processes with the help of an ecosystem of collaborators, including top Silicon Valley entrepreneurs, investors, and the Hasso Plattner Institute of Design at Stanford. The class proved more successful and inspirational than we could have anticipated. Not only did it demonstrate that people are clamoring for ways to use social media for social good, but it confirmed our belief that there is a replicable framework that will allow them to execute their goals efficiently and effectively and to achieve meaningful change.

Most of us have experienced how social technologies are changing the way people relate to each other. They allow us to connect with old friends (and make new ones), share our interests with a broad network of people, and communicate efficiently—often instantaneously. But we are only beginning to understand how these same technologies can fundamentally shift how we engage with and inspire all these networked people and empower them to participate in global movements for change. This book will tell these emerging stories and give you the tools to use social media to make an impact.

Regardless of the change you seek to effect in the world—whether it is to inspire others to join your social movement, mobilize political change, or simply satisfy an individual need—consider this your playbook for moving your cause from awareness to action.

Introduction

Why Reading This Book Is Worth the Investment

A dizzying number of people have written about the mechanics of Facebook, Twitter, email, and YouTube, yet few have addressed one of our strongest motivations: how to leverage the power of the new social media to do something that really matters.

The dragonfly is the only insect able to propel itself in any direction—with tremendous speed and force—when its four wings are working in concert. This ancient, exotic, and benign creature illuminates the importance of integrated effort. It also demonstrates that small actions can create big movements. To us, what we call the Dragonfly Effect is the elegance and efficacy of people who, through the passionate pursuit of their goals, discover that they can make a positive impact disproportionate to their resources. We have been lucky enough to learn from such people and to profile their efforts here.

Most of us are inundated daily with articles, emails, videos, and blog posts. Invitations to participate in compelling social campaigns have become ubiquitous—from Avon's Walk for Breast Cancer, to Pepsi's Refresh campaign, to general appeals to help "save our planet." Yet we glaze over and ignore many, if not most, of these pleas. Or perhaps we join a group, but take no real action on behalf of the cause. Anyone who has ever created a YouTube video, written a blog, or tried to get someone to join a cause on Facebook knows that simply sending out a request doesn't guarantee results.

Yet the power of social technology, when fully engaged, can be nothing short of revolutionary. Just this year, the Red Cross raised more than $40 million for Haiti relief through text message donations. The same technologies that enable us to "poke" our friends or "retweet" an interesting article are the ones that can connect and mobilize us to bring about change. So, what differentiates those who are harnessing social media for something more powerful than fun or procrastination?

It is clear from our research that, in contrast to what you may think, promoting a personal goal is inherently social. To be successful, you must translate your passion into a powerful story and tell it in a way that generates "contagious energy," so that your audience reflects on your tweet, blog post, or email, long after they leave their computers.[1]

By doing this, you generate participation, networking, growth, and ripple effects—forces that combine to form a *movement* that people feel they are a part of. Your personal goal then becomes collective.

Drawing on underlying truths found in psychological research, *The Dragonfly Effect* provides a framework to show you how to do this. In these pages, we will teach you four key skills—Focus, Grab Attention, Engage, and Take Action—which you will use to produce your own colossal results. And we will reveal the secret to cultivating "stickiness," so that your goal is not relegated to Internet oblivion but instead reaches an audience of people who will help propel it forward.

The other reason to read this book is that it might help you become a happier person. Research on happiness makes it clear that happiness, in and of itself, is a bogus conceit. What people *think* makes them happy (moving to sunny California, getting a promotion at work, taking a trip to Disneyland) does not. In fact, the happiest people are those who have stopped chasing happiness and instead search for *meaningfulness,* a change in direction that leads to more sustainable happiness—the kind that enriches their lives, provides purpose, and creates impact.

Why is happiness so elusive? One reason is that the definition of happiness changes every three to five years throughout one's life. The meaning of happiness is not idiosyncratic, individualistic, or random—nor is it singular and stable. Happiness has a clear pattern, indicating that people are pursuing different things across their lifespans.[2] For example, for people roughly ages twenty-five to thirty, money is linked to happiness. After that, meaningfulness starts to outshine it in importance. No matter what age you are now, or what your current priority might be, it's fairly certain that you will at some point be looking for meaningfulness.

Although most people still believe that creating meaning or greater good in the world doesn't align with profit making, we have seen many people and organizations that have created a golden quadrant of "purposeful profit." By aligning the work they love with a profit-oriented business model, they have evolved the organization into something that is much stronger, much more sustainable, and much more effective at generating greater social good.[3]

This is accounted for by a concept known as the *ripple effect.* In economics, the ripple effect is used to show how an individual's increase in spending increases the incomes of others and their subsequent ability to spend. In sociology, it describes how social interactions can affect situations indirectly. In charitable activities, the ripple effect explains how information can

Gap's Give & Get Program

Gap Inc. was one of the first retailers to extend discount privileges to employees' friends and families on special occasions throughout the year. Although originally a fresh idea, these "friends and family days" soon became ubiquitous throughout the industry. Gap wanted to stand out. It also wanted to get back to its roots as an involved and caring member of the communities in which it did business. In the words of founder Doris Fisher, Gap should be "a store with a heart."

This was the impetus for Give & Get, an innovative Web-based cause marketing program that offers customers 30 percent discounts on Gap merchandise—with 5 percent of each sale donated to a designated charity. During this semiannual promotion, employees and customers can download a coupon, which can be redeemed online or at any Gap brick-and-mortar retail store, including Gap, Old Navy, Banana Republic, outlet stores, and Piperlime.

Donations are tracked through unique bar codes in the invitation. One of the key features of the program is that its direction is determined by the employees and customers. They choose which of several designated nonprofit partners they want to support, and in turn their friends and family members, who can share their coupon, are shopping to support their cause. This has resulted in a tremendous commitment and loyalty to the program. The results are impressive. Gap estimates that since it began the Give & Get program in 2008, it has raised $10 million for its nonprofit partners, including such organizations as Teach for America and the Leukemia and Lymphoma Society.

be disseminated and passed from community to community to broaden its impact. In this book, we describe it as the simple idea that small acts can create big change.

Research shows that ripple effects result from small actions that have a positive significant impact on others and over time.

When the action at the epicenter of the ripple effect is based on deep meaning (or something that you believe will make you happy in both a profound and long-lasting way), a multiplier effect can occur.[4]

In such conditions, others around you feel the emotion that you're feeling, and can therefore become more strongly mobilized. This phenomenon whereby emotions you feel infect others is called *emotional contagion.* One view, developed by the psychologist John Cacioppo and his colleagues, is that emotional contagion can be physically manifested by someone's tendency to unconsciously mimic and synchronize facial expressions, postures, and movements with those of another person and, consequently, for the people to converge emotionally.[5] Research has shown that babies often mimic the behaviors of their mothers. People who live with each other for a long period of time grow physically similar in their facial features (by virtue of repeated empathic mimicry).[6] A leader's emotional state can impact the rapport, morale, and even performance of a team or organization.[7] In fact, something as innocuous as the emotional tonality of someone's voice (happy versus sad) can affect how much listeners like a message.[8]

Even more interestingly, in a study of more than forty-seven hundred people who were followed over twenty years, researchers reveal that happiness really is contagious: people who are happy (or become happy) significantly boost the chances that their friends will become happy; and the power of happiness

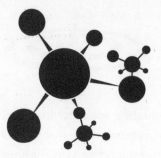

can span up to two more degrees of separation, improving the mood of that person's husband, wife, brother, sister, friend, and even friend's friends. Further, these contagious effects have a lasting impact. One individual's happiness can affect another's for as much as a year. That happiness is more sustained than that which comes from a momentary financial gain. As James Fowler, coauthor of the study, explains, "If your friend's friend becomes happy, that has a bigger impact on your being happy than putting an extra $5,000 in your pocket."[9]

Understanding emotional contagion is important for two reasons. First, that your feelings of happiness or meaning can actually infect others helps explain why some initiatives work and others don't. How did Barack Obama mobilize so many young people in the last U.S. presidential election, even as John McCain had a significantly muted effect (despite running-mate Sarah Palin's brief interjection of high-energy drama)? Why does Kiva, a revolutionary marketplace for microfinance lending to entrepreneurs, successfully empower so many, whereas a similarly spirited (but considerably more rational) product, MicroPlace, hasn't cultivated nearly as large a community, or inspired similar brand recognition? Emotional

[handwritten margin note: Emotional contagion – a key to brand success]

contagion ripples through social networks, and it's important to understand how the contagion of positive emotions can lead others to help.

Second, emotional contagion is pivotal because it underscores the importance of cultivating social good, which is often most resonant with happiness and meaning. And although the idea is not (yet) conventionally accepted, people don't have to give something away for free to do good; they can instead create a business that does good. (Type "social entrepreneur" into Google, and the 15 million hits reveal that this concept has garnered signficant attention.) The for-profit and nonprofit worlds are merging, creating an opportunity for masses of people who drive more profits *and* create greater good.

One example is the for-profit technology company salesforce.com and its innovative integrated philanthropic 1-1-1 model, a vehicle through which the company contributes 1 percent of profits, 1 percent of equity, and 1 percent of employee hours back to the communities it serves. CEO Marc Benioff often talks about the program's secondary gain. "It has made our employees more fulfilled, more productive, and more loyal," he says. "Our customers also have greater appreciation for us because of our philanthropic work. This is not why we do it, but the opportunity to work on something bigger together has positively affected our bottom line."[10]

Before we delve deeper into the blending of for-profit and nonprofit goals, the relationship between happiness and money merits special attention. Our society's prevalent belief is that money will make us happy. However, the reality is that the link between happiness and money is tenuous. Take the striking evidence that although income has steadily increased over

roughly the past fifty years in the United States, life satisfaction has remained virtually flat (a similar pattern is seen in data
from other countries).[11] Yet we continue to overestimate the
impact of income on life satisfaction, and spend our time and
energy trying to grow our wealth.[12] Why is it that the search
for money almost always lets us down? The answer might lie in
the fact that human beings are said to have at least three basic
needs in terms of their sense of self-worth: competence (feeling
that we are effective and able), autonomy (feeling that we are
able to dictate our own behavior), and relatedness (feeling that
we are connected to others).[13] To the extent that a personal or
professional goal does not address these basic needs, the rewards of achieving that goal might be perceived as transient or
lacking.[14] In other words, getting what we want is disappoint-
ing when we aren't wanting what will actually make us happy.

People frequently create wildly inaccurate forecasts of what
will make them happy because they mistakenly associate happiness with short and shallow rewards (as opposed to long-lasting
and deeper rewards). Increasingly, however, research suggests
that individuals become consumers with the goal of "becoming happy" or "getting happier," but that they rarely attain that
goal through their purchases.[15]

It turns out that the adage "money can't buy happiness"
isn't antiquated or false.[16] The results of a recent experiment
showed that spending money on others has a positive impact
on happiness—much more so than spending money on oneself.[17] This was striking given that the participants thought
personal spending would make them happier than spending
on someone else. Eudemonia, or fundamental happiness, is
the result of an active life governed by intrinsic meaning, self-
sacrifice, and self-improvement. Although it all sounds a little

sanctimonious (and conjures images of Gandhi and Mother Teresa), the rewards of bettering the welfare of others have been illustrated by research too many times to simply ignore.

The good news is that all of this research is simple to put into practice. Increasing (and sustaining) your happiness is possible—even easy—if you focus on others (rather than your-self) and on time (rather than money). Research has shown that even thinking about money can have a negative impact on happiness, but that focusing on time increases happiness because it increases interactions and connections with others.[18] Not convinced? Consider the National Institutes of Health study that found that when people are encouraged to think of giving money to a charity, the brain areas usually associated with selfish pleasures are activated.[19] Evolutionarily wired to be prosocial beings, we actually relish giving.

The Dragonfly Effect binds us to others, to larger communities, and to social causes. There really is no better way to strengthen the connection between ourselves and our surroundings, fulfill our psychological and emotional needs, and, above all, create meaning in our lives than by cultivating social good.

The Dragonfly Effect is your road map to doing something purposeful, thoughtful, and well designed. Operating as "social change in a box," it illustrates how synchronized ideas have been used effectively to create rapid transformations—and unveils the secrets to doing just that, step by step, so you can try it too. We'll share how to effectively tap into human behavior, and we'll explain how the four key principles—Focus, Grab Attention, Engage, and Take Action—work. Each of these principles is explored in its own chapter, or wing.

The heart of this book draws on studies on behavior change and the stories of individuals determined to make a difference. You'll gain insight from the founders of eBay's World of Good; storytellers from Pixar; leaders from Facebook, Twitter, and Google; as well as from social entrepreneurs, social media experts, and founders of nonprofit organizations—all of whom use the tools of social media to deliver positive change. We'll study efforts by individual social entrepreneurs who are tapping strategies like viral marketing to empower others to act on their behalf—as well as larger movements, such as how the Obama campaign created political change by leveraging social technology; how the organization Kiva encourages economic justice by making microloans easily available; and how Nike deploys Web tools to harness the volunteer efforts of their thirty-four thousand employees. We'll witness how people like you can achieve a specific goal by using social technologies in ways you may have previously thought to be impossible. Tweeting isn't just sharing about what you ate for breakfast this morning; Facebook isn't just for poking friends. You can leverage these social technologies, strategically and integratively, toward a specific goal that deeply matters to you.

To unpack the information in the text, we offer the Dragonfly Toolkit to provide social media cheat sheets, flowcharts, and boot camps specifically designed for people whose other skills rank ahead of technical proficiency. Dragonfly Frameworks include new models that will help you implement your goal, and Dragonfly Tips are simple, and sometimes unconventional, ideas inspired by consumer marketing research. Expert Insights offer the wisdom of leaders in social media, entrepreneurship, filmmaking, technology, and more, showing how they have uniquely used social media to achieve spectacular results. Throughout you'll find examples of how individuals and groups—on their own or on behalf of corporations—have used specific tools to create impact.

Finally, throughout *The Dragonfly Effect* we will apply concepts from design thinking. Design thinking takes a methodical approach to program and product development. It's taught as a way to create things that are better for the people who will ultimately use them, and helps the creators get over their unintentional biases and misconceptions. Design thinking encourages a human-centric orientation, hypotheses testing, and frequent, rapid prototyping.[20] Time and again, initiatives falter because they're developed with the brand, organization, or cause—rather than *individuals'* needs—foremost in mind. People often tackle a challenge using preconceived notions of individuals' needs and solutions, but deep empathy doesn't guide their decision making, and rapid prototyping is rarely used to solicit feedback. This flawed approach remains the norm in both the business and social sectors. We'll explore compelling examples of where design thinking is implemented throughout this book—and we hope it will inspire you to embrace this way of thinking in your own work.

The Dragonfly Effect is for anyone motivated to act on, propel, and accomplish social good. Whether you're an entrepreneur, an employee of a for-profit company, a volunteer at a nonprofit, or simply an individual trying to improve someone else's life, you can learn about the world of possibility available to you when you leverage social media appropriately. Ultimately, this book demonstrates that you don't need money or power to cause seismic social change. With energy, focus, and a strong wireless signal, anything is possible.

Design Thinking

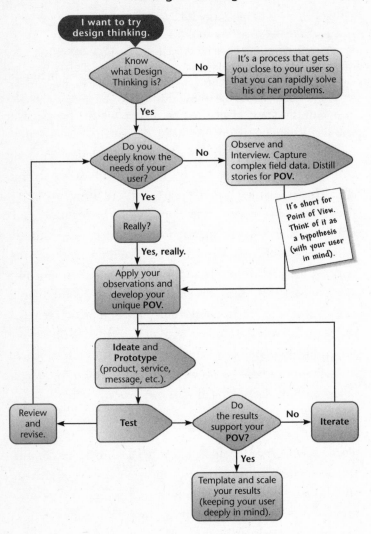

Create Lasting Impact

An integral part of this book is our website www.dragonflyeffect.com, where you'll find a community of people like you, who are harnessing social media to make remarkable impact and sharing their stories, tools, and resources. Via the website, we'll keep you updated on new ways to use the power of social technology to spark social change. The dragonfly has long been a symbol of happiness, new beginnings, and change across cultures. With your help, the Dragonfly Effect will continue to evolve, with ideas, stories, and achievements that it inspires and enables.

THE DRAGONFLY
EFFECT

The Dragonfly Body

The System That Keeps It Airborne

Sameer Bhatia was always good with numbers—and he approached them, as he did everything in his life, from a unique perspective. When the Stanford grad was in his twenties, he came up with an innovative algorithm that formed the foundation of his popular consumer barter marketplace, MonkeyBin. By age thirty-one, the Silicon Valley entrepreneur was running a hot mobile gaming company and was newly married. His friends, who called him Samba, adored his energy, optimism, and passion for pranks. Sameer had an ability to bring out the best in people. With an unrestrained zest for life, he had everything going for him.

Then, on a routine business trip to Mumbai, Sameer, who worked out regularly and always kept himself in peak condition, started to feel under the weather. He lost his appetite and had trouble breathing. He wanted to blame the nausea, fatigue, and racing heartbeat on the humid hundred-degree monsoon weather, but deep inside, he knew something else was wrong.

Sameer visited a doctor at one of Mumbai's leading hospitals, where his blood tests showed that his white blood cell count was wildly out of whack, and there were "blasts" in his cells. His doctor instructed him to leave the country as soon as possible to seek medical treatment closer to home. Immediately upon entering the United States—before he could even make it back to his hometown of Seattle—Sameer was admitted to the Robert Wood Johnson University Hospital in New Jersey. He was diagnosed with acute myelogenous leukemia (AML), a cancer that starts in the bone marrow and is characterized by the rapid growth of abnormal white blood cells that interfere with the production of normal blood cells. AML is the most common acute leukemia affecting adults; it's also very aggressive.

Sameer was facing the toughest challenge of his life. Half of all new cases of leukemia result in death (both in 2008 and today). But Sameer was determined to beat the odds and get better. After Sameer underwent a few months of chemotherapy and other pharmacological treatment, doctors told him that his only remaining treatment option would be a bone marrow transplant—a procedure that requires finding a donor with marrow having the same human leukocyte antigens as the recipient.

Because tissue types are inherited, about 25 to 30 percent of patients are able to find a perfect match with a sibling. The remaining 70 percent must turn to the National Marrow Donor Program (NMDP), a national database with over eight million registered individuals. Patients requiring a transplant are most likely to match a donor of their own ethnicity. That wasn't a promising scenario for Sameer, however. He had a rare gene from his father's side of the family that proved extremely difficult to match. His brother, parents, and all of his cousins were tested, but no one proved to be a close match. Even more worrisome was that of the millions of registered donors in the

NMDP, only 1.4 percent were South Asian. As a result, the odds of Sameer finding a perfect match were only one in twenty thousand. (A Caucasian person has a one-in-fifteen chance.) Worse, there were few other places to look. One would think that a match could easily be found in India, Sameer's family's country of origin. After all, India is the world's second-most populous country with nearly 1.2 billion people. But India did not have a comprehensive bone marrow registry. Not a single match surfaced anywhere.

✄

People often ask what they can do to help in harrowing times. The answer is hard to find. Do you offer to drop off a meal? Lend an empathic ear? Such overtures are well intentioned, but rarely satiate the person who wants to help or the person who needs the help.

Sameer's circle of friends, a group of young and driven entrepreneurs and professionals, reacted to the news of Sameer's diagnosis with an unconventional approach. "We realized our choices were between doing something, anything, and doing something seismic," says Robert Chatwani, Sameer's best friend and business partner. Collectively, they decided they would attack Sameer's sickness as they would any business challenge. It came down to running the numbers. If they campaigned for Sameer and held bone marrow drives throughout the country, they could increase the number of South Asians in the registry. The only challenge was that to play the odds and find a match that would save his life, they had to register twenty thousand South Asians. The only problem: doctors told them that they had a matter of weeks to do so.

Sameer's friends and family needed to work fast, and they needed to scale. Their strategy: tap the power of the Internet and focus on the tight-knit South Asian community to get twenty thousand South Asians into the bone marrow registry, immediately. One of Robert's first steps was to write an email, detailing their challenge and ending with a clear call to action. In the message, he did not ask for help; he simply told people what was needed of them. Because this was the first outbound message broadcasting Sameer's situation, Robert spent hours crafting the email, ensuring that every word was perfect and that the email itself was personal, informative, and direct. Finally, he was ready to send it out to a few hundred people in Sameer's network of friends and professional colleagues.

Dear Friends,

Please take a moment to read this e-mail. My friend, Sameer Bhatia, has been diagnosed with Acute Myelogenous Leukemia (AML), which is a cancer of the blood. He is in urgent need of a bone marrow transplant. Sameer is a Silicon Valley entrepreneur, is 31 years old, and got married last year. His diagnosis was confirmed just weeks ago and caught us all by surprise given that he has always been in peak condition.

Sameer, a Stanford alum, is known to many for his efforts in launching the American India Foundation, Project DOSTI, TiE (Chicago), a microfinance fund, and other causes focused on helping others. Now he urgently needs our help in giving him a new lease on life. *He is undergoing chemotherapy at present but needs a bone marrow transplant to sustain beyond the next few months.*

Fortunately, you can help. Let's use the power of the Net to save a life.

Three Things You Can Do

1. Please get registered. Getting registered is quick and requires a simple cheek swab (2 minutes of your time) and filling out some forms (5 minutes of your time). Registering and even donating if you're ever selected is VERY simple. Please see the list of locations here: http://www.helpvinay.org/dp/index.php?q=event.

2. Spread the word. Please share this e-mail message with at least 10 people (particularly South Asians), and ask them to do the same. Please point your friends to the local drives and ask them to get registered. If you can, sponsor a drive at your company or in your community. *Drives need to take place in the next 2–3 weeks to be of help to Sameer.* Please use the power of your address book and the web to spread this message—today more than ever before, we can achieve broad scale and be part of a large online movement to save lives.

3. Learn more. To learn more, please visit http://www.nickmyers .com/helpsameer. The site includes more details on how to organize your own drive, valuable information about AML, plus FAQs on registering. Please visit http://www.helpvinay.org/ dp/index.php?q=node/108 for more information on the cities where more help is needed. Another past success story from our community is that of Pia Awal; please read about her successful fight against AML at www.matchpia.org.

Thank you for getting registered to help Sameer and others win their fight against leukemia—and for helping others who may face blood cancers in the future.

Truly, Robert[1]

Robert sent the email to Sameer's closest friends and business colleagues—about four hundred to five hundred members of their "ecosystem," including fellow entrepreneurs, investors, South Asian relatives, and college friends. And that set of friends forwarded the email to their personal networks, and on the message spread virally from there. Within forty-eight hours, the email had reached 35,000 people and the Help Sameer campaign had begun.

Sameer's friends soon learned that yet another man in their ecosystem had recently been diagnosed with the same disease: Vinay Chakravarthy, a Boston-based twenty-eight-year-old physician. Sameer's friends immediately partnered with Team Vinay, an inspiring group of people who shared the same goal as Team Sameer. Together, they harnessed Web 2.0 social media platforms and services like Facebook, Google Apps, and YouTube to collectively campaign and hold bone marrow drives all over the country.

Their goal was clear, and their campaign was under way. Within weeks, in addition to the national drives, Team Sameer

---

How to Write an Email That Inspires Action and Spurs Change

Emails must be specific and action-oriented: informing people about the situation, telling them what they can do, and asking them to spread the message even further.

- **Make it personal.** Include accessible and specific details about the person or cause you're trying to help. Give someone a reason to care.

- **Make it informative.** Use email as an opportunity to educate your audience.

- **Make it direct.** Specifically ask the recipients for help, tell them what you want them to do, and give them all the tools they need to do it easily.

and Team Vinay coordinated bone marrow drives at over fifteen Bay Area companies, including Cisco, Google, Intel, Oracle, eBay, PayPal, Yahoo!, and Genentech. Volunteers on the East Coast started using the documents and collateral that the teams developed. After eleven weeks of focused efforts that included 480 bone marrow drives, 24,611 new people were registered. The teams recruited thirty-five hundred volunteers, achieved more than one million media impressions, and garnered 150,000 visitors to the websites. "This is the biggest campaign we've ever been involved with," said Asia Blume of the Asian American Donor Program. "Other patients might register maybe a thousand donors. We never imagined that this campaign would blow up to this extent." Nor did anyone imagine that this campaign would change the way future bone marrow drives are conducted.

Perhaps the most critical result associated with the campaign, however, was the discovery of two matches: one for Vinay, one for Sameer. In August 2007—only a few months after the kick-off of the campaign—Vinay found a close match. Two weeks later, Sameer was notified of the discovery of a perfect (10 of 10) match. Given the timing of when the donors entered the database, it's believed that both Vinay's and Sameer's matches were direct results of the campaigns. Furthermore, it was clear that Sameer and Vinay would not have found matches the traditional way. It takes four to six weeks for a new registrant from a drive to show up in the national database, so they would have needed many more than twenty thousand new registrants to have a statistical chance at a match in such a short time. As Sameer wrote on his blog, "Finding a match through this process in the time required would be nearly *impossible*. Yet many hundreds of hands and hearts around the nation united behind this cause. . . . You all have given me a new lease on life and for that I don't have adequate words to thank you."[2]

Perhaps even more incredible, however, was that the impact of Team Sameer and Team Vinay did not stop with just Sameer and Vinay. Ultimately, they educated a population about the value of becoming registered donors while also changing the way registries work. Above all, they came up with a blueprint for saving lives—one that could be replicated.

The Dragonfly Effect at Work

How did Team Sameer achieve, in the words of Robert Chat-wani, "something seismic"? They didn't set out to help design a system that could be easily, efficiently, and effectively repeated. They just wanted to save their friend's life. But in exceeding the goal by registering 24,611 South Asians into the NMDP registry in eleven weeks, Robert and the team uncovered a process that can be applied to achieve any goal. The effectiveness of the effort can be traced to four steps or principles—Focus, Grab Attention, Engage, and Take Action. To keep it simple, think of the mnemonic Focus + GET.

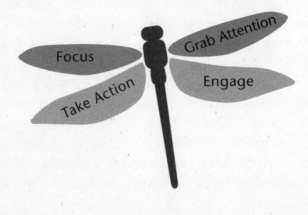

The Dragonfly Model

Focus + GET

The Dragonfly Effect relies on four distinct wings; when working together, they achieve remarkable results.

Focus. Identify a single concrete and measurable goal.

+

Grab Attention. Make someone look. Cut through the noise of social media with something personal, unexpected, visceral, and visual.

Engage. Create a personal connection, accessing higher emotions through deep empathy, authenticity, and telling a story. Engaging is about empowering the audience to care enough to want to do something themselves.

Take Action. Enable and empower others to take action. To make action easy, you must prototype, deploy, and continuously tweak tools, templates, and programs designed to move audience members from being customers to becoming team members—in other words, furthering the cause and the change beyond themselves.

A dragonfly travels with speed and directionality only when all four of its wings are moving in harmony. Metaphorically, then, the central body of the dragonfly should embody the heart and soul of the concept or person you are aiming to help.

To understand how Team Sameer was so effective, consider each of these principles: Focus, Grab Attention, Engage, and Take Action. First, the team *focused* sharply by concentrating exclusively on a single goal. It wasn't hard. The doctors were clear. The chances of finding a bone marrow match were one in twenty thousand. The team needed to get at least twenty thousand South Asians in the bone marrow registry within weeks.

But they didn't get lost in the size of the challenge. They didn't try to sign up every single South Asian in the Bay Area. Instead they focused on those who were well connected to others (for network effects), those who were parents (who could envision their children battling a similar challenge), and those who could relate to Sameer and his story. Those types of individuals were easy to identify, and the scope of the challenge quickly came into focus.

Second, Team Sameer *grabbed attention* by empathizing with their donor audience, relying on photos, making the messages compelling and personal. They also mixed media, employing social media (blogs, video, viral email, Facebook, widgets, pledge lists) as well as traditional media (public relations, television, magazine, telemarketing, posters, and newspapers) and leveraged relationships with celebrities and luminaries. (Then-senator Barack Obama wrote a note in support of the cause, simply because a friend of Vinay's asked him.)

Third, Team Sameer *engaged* deeply with others by making Sameer knowable, telling his story authentically and vividly through video and blog entries, so his story became personally meaningful—even to strangers. The team used targeted messaging to help audiences see themselves in Sameer. Some messages focused on Sameer's South Asian background; others highlighted his youth, newlywed status, or his professional pursuits as a technology entrepreneur.

Team Sameer and Vinay built out a website that acted as a repository for stories, updates, information, and feedback (http://www.helpsameer.org/strategy/). Here volunteers could download materials from a menu including Fliers, Literature, or How to Create a Video. There was even a downloadable how-to guide called "Hosting a Bone Marrow Drive at Work," a Word document with simple instructions and sample emails

Harnessing the Power of Blogging

Sameer and Vinay both blogged throughout the course of their illnesses, and this served as a critical brand-building force for both teams. The blogs created a human connection and proved to be an easy, efficient, and authentic way to circulate the message.

Get the person you are trying to help to write. Successful blogs rest on the personality the author presents and the information that is shared. Sameer was a prolific, passionate, and spirited blogger. "Initially it took some convincing to get Sameer to blog, but when he started to write, his personal story truly emerged. It was a whole new sort of thrust to the campaign, because people could hear his voice," says Robert. "That was powerful." If your subject isn't a single individual or isn't available to blog, embody or act as proxy for the cause in the posts, using "I" statements as much as possible.

Be authentic. Take advantage of authentic characteristics of your cause as they present themselves. Your audience will be drawn to people and personalities that they identify with or that complement them. Vinay and Sameer had different blogging styles and stayed true to what felt natural to them personally. Vinay was more reserved, laid back, and so his team consciously made his site more of an "everyman" brand, "so everyone who read his blog could identify with him," according to Priti Radhakrishnan, Vinay's childhood best friend. "Sameer was more open, and said, 'Put me out there, talk about me, tell me what you need me to do,'" says Robert.

Use the blog as a platform to take a stand and incite action. Sameer wrote on his blog, "South Asians who have taken the trouble to register as donors only step up 30 to 40 percent of the time when called upon as a match. I hope we can all reflect on that number for a second and realize how despicable it is. . . . Our enemy here is part fear, part ignorance, and partly this remnant survivalist desi [a colloquial name for people of South Asian descent] instinct where us Indians will only help our own flesh and blood."[3]

that could be customized by others as needed. The team provided links to downloadable PDFs of the family's appeal, a Tell-a-Friend link that led to Vinay's website, email templates that people could send to their friends, footer templates that people could add to their email signatures, banners to put on blogs or websites, and videos that people could add to their own Facebook pages. Team Vinay worked with Team Sameer to leverage each of these assets by linking and feeding communication across teams, essentially creating one big campaign.

Fourth, Team Sameer enabled others to *take action* by creating a clear and easy-to-execute "call to action" in all communication materials. For example, the call to action was abundantly clear on the website. An online calendar listed donor drives while the text on the welcome page nudged, "Hey visitor, have you already registered?" The site also hosted content that walked people through each step of holding a bone marrow drive, or even what individuals could expect when they attended a drive as a donor. Team Sameer further fueled its call by tracking metrics and collective impact and then feeding those results back to its members, a community of friends, family members, and strangers.

Although certain tasks needed to be coordinated "top down," many did not. The leaders broke off anything that didn't require top-down leadership and empowered (and encouraged) individuals to take action on their own. Communications across the team to share best practices were also important, and using tools such as Google Groups to facilitate those communications proved critical—allowing both groups to move ahead with agility and speed.

"We often tried to think of the traditional way to do something and considered what would happen if we did the exact

opposite—reversing the rules," says Robert. "We weren't wed-
ded to a right way of moving ahead. We just moved ahead.
And we empowered others to move ahead just as quickly." As
Team Sameer member Sundeep Ahuja explains, "We believed
in 'act first, then think.'" When one of their ideas was successful, they would focus on putting more energy and time into
that winning idea. For example, once they saw that corporate
workplace drives were effective, they continued with that and
didn't think of much else. They put some banners on their site
and soon noticed that they weren't yielding registrations, so
they didn't invest further in that effort. "Our motto was try,
abandon, move on, try, abandon, move on . . ."

Although each wing was important individually, it was the
integrated impact of the four wings working in concert that
led to Team Sameer's disproportionate results. None of these
methods would have been effective without the prior, contributing impact of the other steps driving the audience toward
becoming active participants.

Sameer's transplant was completed in fall 2007. One day before
getting his transplant, Sameer's blog reflected optimism and his
usual sense of humor (plus his love of emoticons): "I consider
myself to be extremely lucky. I've had near normal energy levels
and no pain or discomfort. . . . Until then, we are enjoying ☹
the hospital food, trying to return phone calls from friends,
and continuing to get some work done. Oh, and in case you
were wondering, the reason cancer patients are bald is to maximize their Kissable Surface Area (KSA)! Isn't that obvious?? ☺"

Sameer also posted pictures and videos of his bone marrow transplant on YouTube. The videos consisted of small bits

of different parts of the procedure, with the first clip showing him anxiously looking at the bag of bone marrow and
touching it while looking for his name. Sameer's father tells
him not to move it around too much, to which Sameer laughs
and responds, "Don't move it around too much? These cells
were just shipped across the country and made it through bag-
gage claim!" Another part shows Sameer holding the tube and
watching as the bone marrow cells find their way into his body.

Three months after the transplant, just a few days before Christmas 2007, Sameer relapsed. In typical Sameer fashion, he was
back to blogging by December 26. "I don't believe in setbacks,"
he wrote. "We must grow from this experience, whatever
pains—physical and emotional—it brings us. What else, after
all, is the process of life if not growth?"

After several additional setbacks and a valiant fight, Sameer passed away in March 2008. Friends and family mourned
with a memorial service, delivered via a live webcast, which was
attended by more than five hundred people throughout the
world, some of whom knew Sameer and some of whom did
not—all of whom were touched by his story.

The service was recorded and posted on Google Video.
Several thousand people viewed the memorial in the first seven
weeks after his passing. Sameer's memorial photo slideshow,
which joyfully depicts his commitment to his culture, family,
and friends (and his penchant for costumes, including plaid
skirts) was viewed over 6,000 times as well. "We knew that
there were thousands of people around the world that couldn't
be with us, so we put everything online," says Robert. "The
idea that we could use technology to break down barriers and

boundaries was very powerful. It was our way of connecting Sameer's friends and family from around the world to his memorial, which was a celebration of his life."

The week that Sameer died, Vinay, who had received his transplant and made it to the hundred-day mark (what patients aim for so as to be in the clear), was admitted to the ICU. Vinay fought for several months, undergoing chemotherapy and alternative drug treatments. Despite his courage, and the global effort to save his life, Vinay passed away in June 2008.

That's not the end of their stories, though. Their legacy, and their movement, continued to grow worldwide.

※

Through an integrated strategy that leveraged technology, passion, and persistence, as well as an understanding that they couldn't succeed without the help of others, Team Sameer and Team Vinay together reached their goals of registering more than twenty thousand donors and finding a match for both men. Beyond the teams' success in rapidly registering mass numbers of donors, they would ultimately inspire many others and save many other lives. From the base of seventy-five hundred people who registered in the Bay Area, where Sameer lived, eighty additional matches for other leukemia patients were discovered within a year. In 2008 alone, through the efforts of the two teams, 266 other individuals surfaced as matches and donated bone marrow.

Further, the campaign nearly doubled the number of South Asians registered with the NMDP, and retention rates for South Asians have improved to 50 percent, according to Asia Blume of the Asian American Donor Program. Moreover, the campaigns inspired others to change their perception about donating, and that alone has changed lives. Pharmacy student Rina Mehta heard about Team Sameer and Team Vinay from a friend who sent her an invitation through Facebook along with information about a drive in Fremont, California. "It was so easy to register that I decided to do it, and I told everyone I knew to do the same, including my parents," says Rina. Within six months, she received a phone call from the donor program requesting that she come in for more testing, as she was a potential match for another patient. Rina became a peripheral blood stem cell donor to an eighteen-year-old male leukemia patient. "I decided to donate because my fear and any inconvenience it might cause me paled in comparison to what he was going through."

Perhaps the greatest legacy, however, spans far beyond leukemia and marrow donation. The story of Sameer and Vinay is one with a remarkable impact: it shows how the technologies we have at our fingertips can enable us to share stories, mobilize support, and take action to change lives. The two teams started a revolution that can be passed on to others who face similar situations. "We want to give people everything that we did so they can just plug into it, use it, and add onto it," says Dayal Gaitonde, one of Sameer's closest friends and a key member of Team Sameer. "We're looking to open source everything that we did to help others in similar situations."[4]

Big revolutions start with simple ideas and ordinary people. "The notion that there are constraints becomes irrelevant. The biggest asset you have is the ability to think clearly, then take a very big idea and run with it," says Robert.

Lessons from Team Sameer and Team Vinay

How to Do Something Seismic—and Create a Movement

By Robert Chatwani

1. Stay focused; develop a single goal.
2. Tell your story.
3. Act, then think.
4. Design for collaboration.
5. Employ empowerment marketing.
6. Measure one metric.
7. Try, fail, try again, succeed.
8. Don't ask for help; require it.

Now that you've seen the Dragonfly Effect in action, it's time to break it down and show you how to make it work for you. In the next chapter, we'll start with the first wing (skill): Focus.

WING 1
Focus

How to Hatch a Goal That Will Make an Impact

To change the world, you have to get your head together first.
—JIMI HENDRIX

In 2008, thirty-something Colombian engineer Oscar Morales logged on to Facebook to begin organizing a protest against the Revolutionary Armed Forces in his country. Within a week, he had mobilized more than a million people, generated publicity for the release of hundreds of hostages, and incited the largest mass demonstration in the country's history. On another continent, Areej Khan, a young Saudi woman studying art in New York, tapped YouTube, Flickr, and Facebook to spur the government to consider lifting a ban on women drivers in the kingdom. And, in the United States, in an effort in which you might have participated, Barack Obama, at the time a junior senator from Illinois, fueled an online grassroots campaign that led directly to his becoming the first African American president of the United States (and the most popular living figure on Facebook).

A decade ago, it would have been technically impossible for ordinary citizens to respond publicly to global events and share their opinions easily with such a wide audience. It would have been unreasonable to expect that their ideas could inspire that audience to take action and achieve results. Yet that's exactly what happened. We are living in a dramatically smaller and more interconnected world. Practically anyone, anywhere, can capitalize on incredible networking tools that are both free and easy to master.

Although social networking tools are widely used to incite action, the people who have used them most effectively have one thing in common: a laser-like focus. As big, daunting, and impressive as some of their movements seem—citizens rallying against guerrillas, a once-voiceless population protesting for women's rights—each started small, with a few people and a goal.

This chapter, Wing 1, will demonstrate the importance of setting a single focused goal to provide direction, motivation, and operational guidance. A focused goal comprises several elements, which we've broken down into five design principles that can be remembered by the mnemonic HATCH (Humanistic, Actionable, Testable, Clarity, Happiness). The first half of this chapter provides research and case studies that demonstrate how each principle plays a crucial role in successful goal setting. In the second half, we will show how they work together, through an in-depth case study of President Obama's use of social media in his campaign for the White House.

Design Principles to Think Focused

Design Principle 1: Humanistic

Staying focused on your audience may sound basic, but in practice, most of us are easily distracted. Business leaders, non-profit organization directors, and political officials usually draft a "plan of action" that is finalized before any action is taken, and it is typically viewed as the silver bullet for success. Getting everyone on board is paramount; deviation from the plan is discouraged. This type of strategy assumes an ability to predict and navigate all potential outcomes. The problem is, it rarely works. Some uncomfortable truths: you can only guess what will happen in the future; you cannot control outcomes. Those who are willing to test their hypotheses before committing to a detailed approach are more likely to succeed.

The concept of design thinking has become widespread. Businesses including General Electric and Procter & Gamble now strive to take an open-minded and holistic approach to product development that places more emphasis on understanding the needs of the end user. Nonprofits like Vision-Spring, which sells inexpensive reading glasses, are using the

Human Centered Design Toolkit by one of the leading design consultancies, IDEO.[1] Moving fluidly from observation to conceptualization to experimentation to experience (in the form of innovative solutions),[2] VisionSpring was able to make its vision tests more friendly to children—and ultimately reach more people. The Gates Foundation also worked with IDEO's toolkit to help charities develop new programs in collaboration with their beneficiaries.[3]

Although design has historically been associated with creating aesthetically attractive products and technologies, leaders are increasingly applying design thinking at all phases of development as a means of gaining competitive advantage.[4] As Steve Jobs says, "Design is not how things look; it's how things work."

One compelling example of humanistic design thinking in action is the Montana Meth Project, a nonprofit effort whose research-based marketing campaign significantly reduced methamphetamine use in Montana. The project was conceived and backed by software entrepreneur Thomas Siebel, a part-time resident of Montana. He first learned about the state's drug problem from the local sheriff, who told him that nearly all of his

Embrace: How Design Thinking Works

Embrace, a nonprofit organization, was started by a group of Stanford students in the Entrepreneurial Design for Extreme Affordability class at the Hasso Plattner Institute of Design (extreme .stanford.edu). The students were challenged to design a better incubator for the developing world. Each year, twenty million premature and low-birth-weight babies are born, and mortality for these infants is particularly high because most hospitals and clinics in developing countries don't have enough incubators. New incubators cost more than $20,000 each—and donated incubators are confusing to operate, maintain, and repair. Most groups previously aiming to tackle this problem have tried to lower the costs of the incubators, but the Stanford team took an entirely different approach.

The Embrace team began in Kathmandu, the capital city of Nepal. After spending several days observing the neonatal unit of the Kathmandu hospital, the team asked to be taken outside the city to see how premature infants were cared for in rural areas. They learned that the majority of premature infants were born in these rural areas and that most of them would never make it to a hospital. They realized that to save the maximum number of lives, their design would have to function in a rural environment. It would have to work without electricity and be transportable, intuitive, sanitizable, culturally appropriate, and inexpensive.

The team created multiple prototypes that led to the Embrace "Infant Warmer" (embraceglobal.org). The design looks like a sleeping bag, and contains a pouch of phase-change material to keep a baby's body at the right temperature for up to four hours. It can be "recharged" in boiling water in a matter of minutes, which is also how it is sanitized. The Infant Warmer is far more intuitive to use than traditional incubators, and fits well into the culture's recommended practice of "kangaroo care," where a mother holds her baby against her skin. This invention is similar in theory to the pouches skiers use to keep their hands warm, but these portable and electricity-free incubators save infants' lives—and cost only $25.

Embrace has the potential to save more than fifteen million babies in the next ten years. The nonprofit is now manufacturing infant warmers in India, where 40 percent of the world's low-birth-weight infants are born, and the group plans to take the idea worldwide. Embrace is utilizing social media, including online videos and social networks, to mobilize mothers in the developing world to help evangelize their mission.

department's time was spent busting meth labs. Between 1992 and 2002, meth-related hospital admissions rose 520 percent. By 2005, over half of the children in foster care were there because of meth, and half of inmates were incarcerated for meth.[5]

"It occurred to me that perhaps we could look at this as a consumer marketing problem," said Siebel. Meth may be an illegal substance, but like a consumer product, it is readily available, affordably priced, and efficiently distributed. Further, many of its effects, such as weight loss and energy boosting, are perceived as attractive. The Montana Meth Project took a new approach: It sought to publicize the dark side of this product and to "unsell" it.[6]

First, the project heavily researched meth's consumers, determining who they were, what they cared about, and how to reach them. The campaign team began with a baseline survey of more than a thousand respondents, who were twelve to twenty-four years old. A third of consumers had been offered meth within the past year, and almost a quarter saw little or no risk in trying it. The campaign team interviewed drug counselors, a recovering addict, and two teens with family members who were addicts, and conducted focus groups. Their research uncovered something critical: their anticipated target audience, eighteen- to twenty-four-year-olds, were too old, as most teens were forming opinions about drugs around the age of thirteen.

The team developed a number of ads with different characters and messages and tested them with teens. It immediately became clear that the target audience didn't want to hear from adults sharing statistics or their stories. They wanted to hear from kids their own age, people who looked like their friends. The message "not even once" resonated most. The team focused its entire campaign on that slogan.

Some of the ads (see them on YouTube), so graphic they were only shown at night, succeeded in shocking their audience. According to a report by Mike McGrath, Montana's attorney general at the time, methamphetamine-related crime fell 53 percent during the project's first year. A statewide survey revealed that 96 percent of parents had discussed the drug with their children in the past year, up more than 13 percent since the ads began, and more than half said that the campaign had prompted those discussions. In just two years, teen meth use declined 63 percent.

Cultivating a Human-Centered Approach

Before you can involve your audience members, you need to understand them and connect with them as individuals. Start by answering the following questions:

What is she like? Listen, observe, ask questions. Empathize, understand, then keep the face of that individual in mind, using her as a filter for decision making.

What keeps her up at night? Everyone has a fear. What is hers? Can you address it?

What do you want her to do? State this clearly, and make sure the answer is something she cares about.

How might she resist? What will keep her from adopting your message and carrying out your call to action? Identify three bridges you can build:

- *Shared experiences:* What do you have in common: memories, historical events, interests?
- *Shared values:* What do you value personally and collectively: beliefs, norms, and driving desires?
- *Shared goals:* Where are you headed in the future? What outcomes are mutually desired?

The Montana Meth Project succeeded in its goal to unsell meth, illustrating the importance of focusing on the needs of your audience to create broad change. Although the campaign was aimed at teenagers, it also reduced adult meth use by 72 percent and meth-related crime by 62 percent, and moved the state of Montana from the fifth-highest rate of meth abuse in the nation to the thirty-ninth. Arizona, California, Iowa, and other states have since launched their own Meth Projects with spots borrowed from Montana. And, through the Internet, the ads have been viewed by hundreds of thousands of people who have spread them virally, with no airtime costs.

Design Principle 2: Actionable

Striking the right balance between visionary and realistic goals is key to maintaining focus. Goals that are too easy to reach will not satisfy participants and will underdeliver for your cause. Goals that feel out of reach can discourage people, leading them to quit easily or not to try at all. To achieve balance, break the goal down into parts: a single long-term macro goal and a number of short-term process goals, or micro goals.

At the beginning, don't focus on that long-term macro goal. Instead, focus on your tactical micro goals so that you will have a clear sense of progress. Imagining the *process* of reaching a goal (for example, studying hard for an exam) is more effective than envisioning the outcome (getting an A).[7] Pursuing actionable micro goals reduces a complex problem into something that is manageable.[8] In other words: small micro goals not only mark progress but also keep you sane and reduce stress.

Understanding Macro Goals
and Tactical Micro Goals

Macro goal: a long-term goal that identifies the problem, the "gap" you intend to close. A macro goal carries belief and feeling. Things to consider: it should define the brand behind the project, and what types of connections the team is seeking to create (social, potential consumer segments, seeking funds, creating awareness).

Tactical micro goal: a short-term goal that is small, actionable, and measurable. It can be an approximation or first step for achieving your larger goal.[9] Things to consider: developing the brand, defining specific audience segments, creating a dialogue with end users.

In their book *Nudge,* Richard Thaler and Cass Sustein argue that although one might think that high stakes attached to a goal would make people pay more attention, they actually just make people tense.[10] High stakes attached to big goals often induce people to feel stress, and in turn they do nothing to achieve the goal (and hence seemingly abandon their rationality). Consider, for example, how one might handle the goal "to become healthy." Where to start? Abandon late-night snacking? Start hitting the gym? Choose salad over pizza for lunch? Chasing all these solutions quickly becomes overwhelming. Too big a gap between the current state and the desired state (being unhealthy versus becoming healthy) often leads to discouragement and goal abandonment.[11]

If a micro goal is set—for example, to run thirty minutes a day around the lake—it's more achievable, and the person who pursues it will be working toward the macro goal of becoming healthier. The positive feedback he receives will encourage him to take the next step. Narrow, proximal (short-term) goals lead to better performance because they can promote our feelings of competence[12] and increase the chance that we will enjoy tasks.[13]

There is another benefit to honing your larger single goal into smaller micro goals. A growing amount of research shows that, more generally, small is not inconsequential. For example, psychological studies have shown that first impressions based on micro amounts of information are surprisingly accurate. In one study, teachers' effectiveness was accurately predicted based solely on six-second clips.[14]

The principle of micro changes also guides decision making. For example, the order in which food items are listed on a menu affects customers' decisions. In one experiment, simply rearranging the order of a dish on a menu yielded a change in the consumption of some items by as much as 25 percent.[15] In another example, *how* companies present savings plan options to employees affects employees' decisions. Automatic enrollment in 401(k) savings plans leads to significantly higher participation, which is surprisingly low in the absence of automatic enrollment, despite considerable benefits.[16]

Noting that people often make suboptimal decisions in reality, behavioral economists have pointed to the role of *choice architecture*, or how you set up a choice, to affect which decisions are made.[17] With the right approach, we each have the power to help people make better decisions—and effect big changes one small step at a time.

Design Principle 3: Testable

Be sure your goal is testable. There's no easy way to measure something as complex as a cure for cancer or the achievement of world peace, but you can measure the number of people who register to donate bone marrow, or the number of people who show up to a protest and the number of press articles it receives, or the number of votes in an election. Establish metrics to ensure progress. Combining goal setting and feedback is more effective than goal setting alone.[18]

Use Metrics to Test the Validity of a Goal

As Chris Anderson advises in *The Long Tail,* don't predict—measure and respond. Although your goal should be specific and concrete, you need to be able to tweak it as necessary along the way, based on what you learn as you monitor your progress.

Making Data-Driven Decisions: How to Test the Success of Your Site

*By **Avinash Kaushik**, author of* Web Analytics 2.0

- **Don't get enamored by shininess.** Instead, think about measures such as bounce rate (the percentage of visitors who "bounce" away from your site after arriving at the landing page), then use analytics and data to strip features away to make bad sites better.

- **Clearly define quantifiable success metrics.** Learn to focus on micro conversions that add up in the long term to help you achieve your macro goal. Think about how to have your message amplified—your strategy should be to share, not shout.

- **Listen.** Your goal is to understand your audience and identify "segments of discontent." Surveys are a great tool. The best surveys ask three simple questions:
  - Why are you here?
  - Were you able to complete your task?
  - If not, why?

EXPERT INSIGHTS

Set specific deadlines. People perform best when working toward a deadline.[19] Having milestone points along the way enables regimented tracking of progress, which both increases the chance that you can overcome obstacles and allows for course correction.[20] Just as important, having a benchmark maintains optimism, which you'll need in order to stay on course.[21]

Testable goals provide milestones and opportunities to mark your achievements. Psychologists have shown that this approach is most aligned with human preferences for learning, motivation, and perception.[22] Achieving more, smaller successes (as opposed to fewer, larger successes) works as positive reinforcement and sustains momentum. We all think we want a big win, but the reality is that big wins can have unexpected negative consequences. Looking over the top of the mountain can create uncertainty about what comes next and nostalgia for the journey that's now in the past. You see this when a person retires, or when a start-up is acquired and the original team gets lost in the new organization. Further, big wins bring higher expectations and countermeasures, both of which render the next win more difficult to achieve.

Design Principle 4: Clarity

Few pursuits come with built-in finish lines, so you need to construct them yourself. A key design criterion is clarity. Indeed, a clear goal may have multiple dimensions, but pursuing multiple goals is counterproductive, as it causes people to lose focus.[23] Research shows that the reason why many don't achieve their goals is not that they don't try hard enough or think strategically enough, but simply because they embarked on too many goals or set conflicting goals.[24]

Consider this: a Stanford study found that heavy multitaskers actually underperform in mental tasks as compared to light multitaskers.[25] When we are bombarded with multiple sources of information, it's impossible to filter out what's irrelevant. As Tad Williams once said, "A well-aimed spear is worth three."

Highly specific goals promote better performance than general, do-your-best goals. They beget greater satisfaction and, ultimately, a stronger commitment.[26] Why? Nonspecific goals overtax the prefrontal cortex, the brain area largely responsible for willpower. When the prefrontal cortex—which is also responsible for solving abstract problems, keeping us focused, and handling short-term memory—becomes overly occupied, willpower weakens.[27]

ClimateChangeUS offers a good example of how a single clear goal increases an organization's chances of bringing about large-scale change. With the goal to become a trust agent for scientific information on climate change, the group started a Twitter account to raise awareness about the release of the Global Climate Impacts in the United States report in June 2009. It gained traction, and after a few weeks expanded its goal to share the latest peer-reviewed climate science. In just a few weeks, ClimateChangeUS succeeded at its original goal—and established itself as something bigger: a trusted resource for journalists, educators, and citizens. Note that expertise is often transitive; once you establish credibility in one domain and are recognized, people assume you can apply your expertise to other challenges.[28]

Design Principle 5: Happiness

The goal you choose needs to be personally meaningful. The mere thought of achieving it should, at some level, make you happy. If you aren't motivated by something fundamental, others are not going to be, either.

Too often in business the goal is to increase sales or maximize profit, which may be clear but is hardly motivating. Those firms that can get beyond financials to more meaningful goals are more likely to excite employees. Kaiser Health is about helping members thrive; Whole Foods is about making healthy eating pleasurable, and P&G's Pampers is about providing the best care for babies—all meaningful goals with the potential to inspire. If people really care about your goal, they will be more willing to work longer and harder.

Ask yourself whether your goal is personally meaningful. Do you have a compelling backstory? People are unlikely to help unless they know *why* you're doing what you're doing. People who set goals based on personal interests and values achieve those goals more often because they're continually

[handwritten margin notes: Help CKD pts live longer more fulfilling lives / Help hospitals save more lives]

Five Design Principles to Focus

HATCH

Humanistic. Focus on understanding your audience rather than making assumptions about quick solutions.

Actionable. Use short-term tactical micro goals to achieve long-term macro goals.

Testable. Before you launch, identify metrics that will help evaluate your progress and inform your actions. Establish deadlines and celebrate small wins along the way.

Clarity. Keep your goal clear to increase your odds of success and generate momentum.

Happiness. Ensure that your goals are meaningful to you and your audience.

energized and thus stay more focused.[29] If you were to achieve your goal, how would you feel? If you were to fail in achieving it, how would you feel? The answers to these questions should be motivating in their own right.

HATCHed Goals in Action

You will need all five HATCH components to focus your campaign. If one or more is missing or deficient, your task will be that much harder. How will you HATCH your goal? Fill in the chart here and refer to the Help Vinay and Sameer column for examples.

	Help Vinay and Sameer	Your Campaign
Humanistic	Focus on Vinay and Sameer as people who have interests, similarities, and lives that the audience can relate to.	
Actionable	Process goals include getting others to host their own donor drives through empowerment marketing.	
Testable	Number of registrants toward a specific number (20,000) within 6–12 weeks.	
Clarity	Get 20,000 South Asians into the bone marrow registry. (Goal is not clouded with aims to cure cancer or create a registry in India.)	
Happiness	Volunteers and audience are motivated by Sameer's and Vinay's personal stories—and their relevance. Doing something meaningful makes them feel good.	

Too Realistic? (handwritten annotation)

Yes We Can! How Obama
Won with Social Media

Barack Obama's 2008 run for the White House is perhaps the broadest campaign to successfully use social media for social change.[30] Obama's team effectively utilized new social media tools—and according to some experts, this bold move secured him the presidency. Analysts at Edelman Research say that Obama won by "converting everyday people into engaged and empowered volunteers, donors, and advocates through social networks, email advocacy, text messaging, and online video."[31]

Although Obama's grassroots effort was savvy at using a wide variety of existing social media and technology tools, its key channel was MyBarackObama.com (nicknamed MyBO). In many ways this easy-to-use networking website was like a more focused version of Facebook. It allowed Obama supporters to create a profile, build groups, connect and chat with other registered users, find or plan offline events, and raise funds. MyBO also housed such user-generated content as videos, speeches, photos, and how-to guides that allowed people to create their own content—similar to a digital toolbox.[32] The mission, design, and execution of the site echoed the single goal of the grassroots effort: to provide a variety of ways for people to connect and become deeply involved.

The Obama team, which created the most robust set of online tools ever used in a political campaign, did so in less than ten days, timing the site to launch around Obama's presidential campaign announcement. Keeping focused on one clear mission ("involvement through empowerment") helped them not only execute fast but also execute right. In terms of core functionality, MyBO was the same on launch day as it was on Election Day.

It was no coincidence that MyBO shared similarities with Facebook; the Obama campaign had familiarized itself with Facebook early on, first using it before the midterm elections. At that time, Facebook had just started to allow political candidates to build profile pages, and even though Obama wasn't a midterm candidate, he still wanted to harness online momentum. The campaign also hired Facebook cofounder Chris Hughes to help it develop and execute its social media strategy.

Facebook Boot Camp

Lady Gaga, with more than 13 million friends, is the most popular living person on Facebook. Facebook isn't just for people, though; Starbucks, with more than 11 million fans, is a highly networked company. Starbucks uses the site to engage with customers, build excitement for new products, educate fans about such social-good initiatives as buying fair trade coffee, and raise awareness for its Pledge 5 volunteer campaign. How can you leverage this phenomenon?

1. Start with a Facebook page, not just a Facebook group. The differences are subtle, but Facebook pages have different features, such as targeted updates, custom applications, and usage metrics.
2. There's no limit of people who can join your Facebook page, so ask team members as well as friends and family to sign on as early fans. When they do, it will show up in their news feed and help fuel word of mouth.
3. Register for a "vanity URL." You'll need a particular size of fan base to register. Facebook does this to prevent "squatters" taking up every conceivable simple URL.
4. Post videos and pictures from events on the page and tag people in them. Viewers will viscerally engage in a way that is difficult to replicate as quickly with the written word.
5. Be yourself and use your voice. Authenticity is essential to genuinely engage with your community.

Hughes's revolutionary contribution to MyBO was using social media not just to capture people's attention but to enable them to become activists (without a single field staffer telling them how).[33] These activists became a team—initially gathering online and then coordinating offline events to evangelize their cause.

MyBO integrated behavioral truths (involvement leads to commitment; opportunity leads to empowerment) and social media tools to inspire people to participate in ways that they found meaningful and rewarding. MyBarackObama.com was not merely a website; it was a movement that made politics accessible through social media that people were already using every day. It changed the face of political campaigns forever; but, more important, it made getting involved as easy as opening up an Internet browser and creating an online profile. Although Obama's social media team may have achieved the most ambitious and most successful social networking movement to date, its efforts also provide keen insights and simple lessons that can be applied to any campaign, including yours. The following rules are the first steps to executing your focused goal—and maximizing your impact.

Exploit Existing Tools

The Obama campaign not only excelled at creating its own site but also mastered using the free tools that were already available. This is an idea that every effort can borrow.

Instead of focusing on Obama's numbers (which are impressive but intimidating), focus on the power of having these social media imprints out there. Obama's universal social media presence demonstrates that even in the most traditional endeavors, new media matter. His campaign was able to garner

5 million supporters on fifteen different social networks. By November 2008, Obama had approximately 2.5 million (some sources say as many as 3.2 million) Facebook supporters, out-performing Republican opponent John McCain by nearly four times.[34] On Twitter, Obama had more than 115,000 followers, more than twenty-three times more than John McCain. People spent 14 million hours watching campaign-related Obama videos on YouTube, with 50 million viewers total. That was four times the number of McCain's YouTube viewers.[35] "No other candidate has ever integrated the full picture the way [Obama] has, that's what's really new about his campaign,"[36] said Michael Malbin, executive director of the Campaign Finance Institute.

Just creating a profile or fan page isn't enough. It's how you use these tools. One effort in particular, the Dinner with Barack fundraising event, stands out because it tapped many different technologies to achieve its goal—making people feel involved and empowered. Traditional fundraising dinners al-low big donors to buy access to candidates. That didn't reso-nate with the Obama campaign, which instead looked for a way to acknowledge that everyone is an important participant in creating change.

The team selected four donors who had given *any* amount and who had shared their stories about why they were moti-vated to donate. It promoted the unusual effort on MyBO: "While a typical political dinner these days consists of officials being wined and dined by Washington lobbyists and bigwigs from special interest PACs, Barack will be sitting down with four regular people from across the country, who will share their stories and discuss the issues that matter most to them."[37]

Over the course of the campaign, the team hosted two Din-ner with Barack events, broadcasting the events on YouTube and on the campaign's website. Those videos went viral when viewers reposted them on their blogs.

Most important: the tactic inspired others. "The stories put a human face on our donors," says new media director Joe Rospars. They also raised a significant amount of money. "People appreciated that we were doing things in a different way because small donors, especially early ones, sometimes think that the closer you get to the political process, the ickier it gets. But on our organizing mission, we were able to get twenty-five thousand new people to give $5, for example, and . . . provide a huge new list . . . of people who've made some level of commitment to the campaign."

When it comes to philanthropic activities on social media, social networks foster—through greater transparency— closer relationships between donors and causes. For example, on Facebook Causes, Facebook's platform to support activism and fundraising, you can see in detail how money is dispersed. Furthermore, by adding fun, personal, and accessible elements that reduce the distance between the individual and the cause, you can create powerful connections that serve as engines for action and change.

Make the Moments Count

Obama's team celebrated milestones, and basked in the wins along the way. One great example involves their use of email and texts. The campaign was an email production machine, sending out a total of one billion emails. There were more than 8,000 unique e-mail messages targeted to specific segments of its 13-million-member email list, with subjects ranging from state and residence to social issues to donation history. The team

Go Where Your People Are

The Obama campaign invested in social networks, putting profiles for Obama on My Space, Facebook, LinkedIn, Black Planet, Eons, AsianAve, Flickr, Digg, Eventful, FaithBase, GLEE, MiGente, My Batanga, and DNC PartyBuilder, as well as driving traffic to video on the campaign's YouTube channel.

It seems the campaign was everywhere; however, in an effort to remain focused, the campaign limited itself to fifteen external social networks. "These social networks are shopping malls that have millions of people already hanging out in them," says Scott Goodstein, the campaign's external online director. So the question becomes, how to find the people that are going to be your advocates and have them talk about your message? It's no different than basic organizing and going door-to-door anywhere in the country."

Go to the audience you have. The Obama campaign sought out the disabled American community social network, Disaboom. "It was a great way to reach out to the disabled American community and have a real conversation about their issues and questions and point people in the right direction towards our policy papers," says Goodstein.

Go to the audience you want. Obama was also active on the business social network LinkedIn. "This isn't exactly the most progressive of the social networks, mostly comprised of CEOs and large businesses. Statistics showed that it was more Republican, but we went on the site," explains Goodstein. "We asked a question on the site, 'What are your suggestions for helping small business?' And we were actually able to hear from people that ran their own small business about what their real problems are. Then we had President Obama address a couple of the really thought-out suggestions and just engaged in a conversation and dialogue with people that he wouldn't have necessarily met any other way."

Keep the dialogue going. Capitalizing on the novelty of being able to connect with a candidate, Goodstein's team maintained Obama's presence by responding to questions on the sites. Links to the various social networks were posted on MyBO.

created content for the emails and tested it by segmenting email lists, monitoring responses, and adapting their messages on the basis of that feedback. They learned to engage their audience via email and text message, which paid off when they needed to communicate with supporters at the most pivotal moments. On August 23, 2008, Obama's team sent out a text to its one million subscribers announcing that Senator Joe Biden would be Obama's running mate. Nielsen Mobile called it the largest mobile marketing event in the United States to date.[38]

Ultimately, the campaign garnered 3 million mobile and SMS subscribers. On Election Day, supporters received three texts. The final one said, "All of this happened because of you. Thanks, Barack."

The Power of One

When you think about what you'd like to achieve in your project, always think in terms of one person and stay focused on that individual. The Obama campaign stayed focused on Obama. This idea came directly from the way people on the campaign personally connected to Obama. "I connected to Barack as an individual first. It just so happened that he was in politics," Chris Hughes said in an interview with *Fast Company.*

Obama brought that connection to the social Web, which is what was so effective about his campaign, says Randi Zuckerberg, who leads marketing, political, and social change initiatives on Facebook. "One thing that really strikes me about Obama's Facebook page is how authentic he is. He has his favorite music up there, as well as his interests, including basketball and spending time with kids. *Godfather I* and *II* are his favorite movies. His staffers were constantly updating their profiles, telling people they were on the campaign trail, or eating pizza, or stuck in traffic. It was this kind of voice that made everyone feel like they were in one conversation together."

The campaign took similar advantage of YouTube, using the site to introduce its audience to Barack Obama the person. Particularly popular videos include Obama's appearance on *Ellen* (8 million views), his speech on a more perfect union (6 million views), and his "Yes We Can" speech (3 million views). YouTube also afforded the campaign a significant amount of free advertising. Political consultant Joe Trippi told the *New York Times* that the YouTube videos were more effective than television ads because viewers chose to watch them or received them from a friend instead of having their television shows interrupted for something they had no say in. According to Trippi, the 14.5 million hours that viewers spent watching clips on YouTube would have cost $47 million had the content been delivered via broadcast TV.[39]

Using the media to allow people to get to know Obama in this personal way made him more accessible—and that made all the difference for his campaign. This is a lesson that can easily be replicated. Steve Grove, the head of news and politics at YouTube, explains: "There's a tendency to think of new media as a secret sauce that suddenly unlocks this viral potential, and there's truth to that. But there's no such thing as some viewcount fairy dust that the Obama campaign had that somehow made their YouTube videos climb that chart. They had a very talented candidate who was a great communicator and they had a campaign philosophy that matched and mirrored very well with the Internet—openness, inclusiveness, self-organizing, grassroots. If they didn't have that campaign philosophy, they wouldn't have gone anywhere."

The strategy to be more personal has been adopted by other politicians all over the world. Take, for example, French president Nicholas Sarkozy, who is known to spend time tending to his image on his Facebook page (http://www.facebook.com/nicolassarkozy). Not shy about sharing personal details offline, he brought this attitude online, with impressive results. When Sarkozy switched his profile picture from a buttoned-up official image to one that featured him wearing an open shirt with no tie, for example, he landed significantly more fans. Sarkozy further capitalized on the power of getting more personal by adding videos to his Facebook page that depict his more domestic side. One shows him bursting into a room to kiss his wife, Carla Bruni. The supermodel touches his hand, wipes his brow, and calls after him, "Good luck, *mon chouchou*" (my sweet).[40] One of his Facebook photo albums documents a visit with Woody Allen. It has received thousands of "likes" and hundreds of comments. We'll talk more about the influence of celebrities later. For now, the take-away is: focus on one individual and add elements that make him or her accessible—and fun.

And, some final advice: personality is a powerful asset to work with, but approach it with caution. (There's always a risk of revealing too much, which hazards landing you on one of the Internet's many walls of shame, such as regretsy.com). Think carefully about who you are and the ideas and messages you would like to convey.

Small Acts Contribute to Big Changes

We've already introduced the idea that small changes can have ripple effects, creating larger, more profound changes. Identified by management theorist Jacon Kounin in 1970, the ripple effect means that you never know when some small thing you do today could have an impact many years from now.

EXPERT INSIGHTS

Three Tips for Facebook Presence

By **Randi Zuckerberg**, *creative & buzz marketing, politics, and social change at Facebook*

- **Virality.** Virality on Facebook is driven by tagging. Tagged friends and fan pages on shared content appear in users' news feeds, which allows other network members to see and subsequently share it. Lenny Kravitz hires photographers to photograph fans at his concerts, posts the images on his Web site, and allows fans to easily tag themselves—driving traffic to his page.

- **Video.** Make sure you upload the video into Facebook (not just link to YouTube) to keep people on your page and prevent them from going off-site—and getting lost. The live stream of Obama's inauguration within Facebook allowed friends to simultaneously watch the speech and discuss it with their friends.

- **Insights.** With fan page metrics, such as number of hits by region, Facebook allows organizations to understand who and where their constituents are, what they care about, and how to reach them. The result: customer targeting and segmentation like never before.

You might worry that the single focused goal you have in mind, even if you achieve it, is so narrow that it doesn't matter in the grand scheme of things. Think again, because if successful, your goal has ripple potential that could bring about powerful social changes . . . just as the focused goal of Team Sameer to save one life has saved hundreds of lives. Just as precise research for the Montana Meth Project cascaded to other states and reduced teen and adult meth abuse and meth-related crime. Just as the clearly targeted effort of the Obama team has rewritten political history.

The Obama campaign offers a particularly compelling case study in how its focus on inspiring mass involvement or winning people's time (over money and votes) resulted in winning time, money, *and* votes. The secret to this seemingly impossible equation was in staying true to the initial goal as the team evolved its program. The team knew involvement would lead to further commitment, which could create a movement. "When we did our first set of fundraising, our goal was the number of people we wanted giving, not the dollar amount," says Rospars.

Obama raised $639 million from three million donors. Although his campaign did raise some money from well-connected fundraisers, the majority of the $639 million was raised through the Internet.[41] Volunteers on MyBO generated $30 million through their 70,000 personal fundraising pages.[42]

The Obama campaign illustrated the massive, meaningful impact that social media can have on getting young people engaged and involved. How exactly did the organizers use technology to

Jenni Ware and the Power of the Ripple Effect

Jenni Ware was at the grocery checkout when she discovered she had lost her wallet. Carolee Hazard, a complete stranger in line behind her, paid her $207 bill. When Ware paid her back, the check included an extra $93 as thanks.

Hazard posted on Facebook about what had happened and asked friends what they'd do with the extra money. "Give it to charity!" was the response. Touched by Ware's honesty, Hazard matched the $93 and again queried her Facebook friends where to donate the $186.

Soon, friends began donating $93 of their own, and the total quickly grew. This random act of kindness, spread through social networks, turned $93 into more than $30,000 to benefit the Second Harvest Food Bank of Silicon Valley. The amount, which has been given in donations from $.93 to $93, is still growing; Hazard's goal is to raise $93,000.

change the face of campaigning? The campaign didn't simply create a Facebook fan page and a YouTube account and expect things to take off: the team created an energy of involvement, of participation, and a sense of purpose in its supporters, each of which was *funneled* through social networking technologies. The medium wasn't the message, so to speak; it was the vehicle. It connected real people, with real enthusiasm, in real time, and gave them an easy and accessible way to show their support for change. Obama's ever-present campaign slogan was "Change we can believe in." In retrospect, the slogan could have been "Change we can be a part of."

We're just a few short years into a Web 2.0 world, and we've already seen how it's rewritten the rules of the offline world. The first "Internet president" changed the way elections will be run in the future. The Obama campaign team showed us that technology was not just a "tool in the arsenal, but a transformative force," says Jascha Franklin-Hodge, cofounder of Blue State Digital, the new media firm that powered many of the tools behind Obama's site. "The campaign understood the power of the Internet to get people engaged in the process on a scale never done before."[43] And, many agree, the Internet landed Obama the presidency. "Were it not for the Internet, Barack Obama would not be president. Were it not for the Internet, Barack Obama would not have been the [Democratic] nominee," Arianna Huffington, editor-in-chief of the *Huffington Post,* said in the *New York Times.*[44]

Lessons from Obama's Campaign

Present a focused message and vision. Obama focused on three key words: *hope, change, action.*

Map out your digital landscape. Know social influencers, the top bloggers, the top social networks, and the central communications hubs.

Build relationships. Listen, be authentic, and ask questions.

Have a clear call to action. Every action in the Obama campaign was geared toward getting people to vote. The purpose of online activity was to create offline activity.

Empower brand ambassadors. Embrace cocreation; let the brand evolve without you directing all of the evolution.[45]

Getting Started with Focus

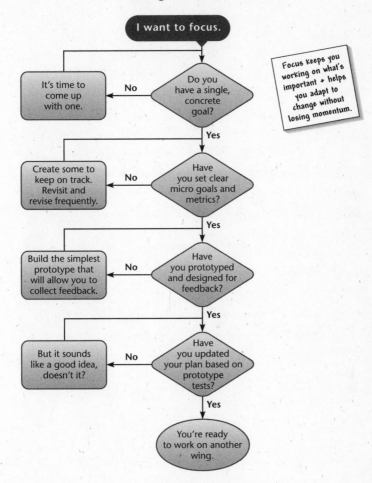

WING 2
Grab Attention

*How to Stick Out in an Overcrowded,
Overmessaged, Noisy World*

This is designed to get somebody's attention. This is a hammer.
—REP. JASON WATKINS

A new clothes retailer on the Web, focused exclusively on designing pants for well-educated, high-income men? The whole world—let alone the fashionistas—should have let out a collective yawn. Instead, Bonobos, founded in 2008, sold $1.8 million in product, nearly breaking even in its first year of operation. In its second year, the company nearly tripled its 2008 revenues, turning a profit in an economic climate in which most clothing retailers were struggling just to survive. What did Bonobos do to spawn such success?

The secret of Bonobos's success was a three-pronged plan that could be adopted by many retailers to grab consumers' attention. First, the founders came up with an idea that was brilliantly simple yet immensely "sticky"—an online store where discriminating men who hated to shop could find well-priced, attractive clothing that actually fit. Men enjoyed the simplicity of the transaction and its inevitable aura of privilege and savvy. Second, to keep costs comparatively low, its direct-to-consumer distribution model bypassed the conventional brick-and-mortar retail channel, minimizing overhead and cutting out middlemen. And third, its Internet- and social network–driven marketing strategy used word of mouth to get directly to the target audience without costly traditional media advertising.

Stickiness refers to a quality that the most successful ideas and endeavors have: that of grabbing and holding attention.[1] It's a concept that grew to maturity during the dot-com era, fueled by Chip and Dan Heath's bestselling book, *Made to Stick: Why Some Ideas Survive and Others Die.* In the case of Bonobos's cofounders Brian Spaly and Andy Dunn, the sticky concept was based on an intuitive feel for what men wanted when shopping for pants. First and foremost was fit. The company's pants were designed to comfortably fit a more muscular physique than most fashionable men's trousers. The branding campaigns they instigated honed in on this unique value and were—in and of themselves—highly differentiated and memorable. For example, their customer service professionals are called "Ninjas" and among other responsibilities, are charged with tweeting for the company.

Bonobos runs creative contests to grab the attention of both existing and potential customers. The company's most notable campaign was Tweet for Trunks. Once a day for a month, CEO Dunn asked questions like, "Should Bonobos make denim?" or "What is an area where we can improve?" and followers who responded were eligible to win a free pair of the company's new swim trunks. The promotion helped the company increase its Twitter follower count by 300 percent, and led to an increase in sales conversions on its site. Such ideas helped Bonobos stand out.

Bonobos even uses its blog to apologize for mistakes. In a viral campaign, Bonobos produced a video called "Big Chimpin'," which featured a dancing chimpanzee. The Big Chimpin' campaign amassed 18,000 views in seventy-two hours on YouTube, but the company was vilified by animal rights activists for using an endangered animal known for being treated poorly by trainers. Bonobos apologized to activists via its blog, admitted that producing the video had been a poor decision, and directed customers to a video on the subject from People for the Ethical Treatment of Animals. (It also used the opportunity to bolster awareness around its commitment to support an ape sanctuary in the Democratic Republic of Congo.)

Grabbing attention, which lies at the heart of stickiness, represents the second wing of the Dragonfly Effect and is the critical follow-up to Focus. Grabbing attention is more than capturing someone's interest for a moment as he scans a page or screen. It's a deeper, more elaborate hook. Whatever it is, it makes people want to know more. And once you've grabbed their attention, amazing things can follow, whether it's getting men who hate to shop to buy more pants, or enticing people to volunteer time or money to a cause. If you have a great idea or cause, you've got your hook. Now for the greater challenge: breaking through today's barrage of noise—from media, the Internet, work, and even family.

The amount of information generated each year—both offline and online—is growing at a rate exceeding 65 percent, according to a 2009 survey by IDC.[2] Survey respondents report that they already spend more than 26 percent of their time dealing with the consequences of information overload. When it comes to marketing and advertising, getting anyone's attention is increasingly difficult. Consumers don't always welcome messages from advertisers—hence the popularity of digital video recorder (DVR) devices that allow people to record their favorite television shows and fast-forward through the commercials when watching them. A 2004 study showed that 65 percent of consumers felt bombarded by advertising messages, and almost as many (60 percent) had a more negative opinion of advertising than even a few years prior. They felt that advertising had nothing relevant to offer them.[3] Not surprisingly, consumer trust in advertisers has declined sharply as well. In 2007, one study found that only 17 percent of consumers said they trusted people who work in the advertising industry, according to mediaVillage.com. (Then came *Mad Men,* which did as much damage as good to the mystique and image of ruthlessness surrounding the advertising industry.) By mid-2009, the proportion of consumers who said they believed marketers' ad claims had plummeted to 6 percent, according to Forrester. The net: a stunning 94 percent of people have turned their backs on traditional advertising.

So whom do people trust instead? Each other. According to the 2009 Nielsen Global Online Consumer Survey of more 25,000 Internet consumers from fifty countries, 90 percent of consumers trust product recommendations from personal acquaintances—making such recommendations the most trusted form of advertising.[4] And now that social media have transformed the business of communication, people can promote (themselves, their favorite haunts, brands, and causes) to their hearts' content, for free, and those on the receiving end can choose to filter them out, which makes the whole enter-prise mind-blowingly effective. This puts social networking—whether done via email, blogs, online communities, or retailer websites themselves—right in the forefront of today's market-ing and advertising wars.

Bonobos was competing in a particularly fierce market in a particularly noisy marketplace. As information-saturated ven-ues go, the Web tops almost any list, with 170 terabytes of in-formation (seventeen times more information than the Library of Congress's print collections). In 2002, people sent more than thirty-one billion email messages every day; by 2006, that number had more than doubled. People—and not just teens—send five billion instant messages (IMs) a day. And texting is quickly catching up: by mid-2009, 203 million Americans were texting 2.5 billion messages per day.[5]

To avoid losing their minds, people have built up immuni-ties to marketing. It doesn't work to simply shout louder. You have to come up with new strategies for grabbing their atten-tion, by understanding their plight and creating a message that speaks to them.

In the case of Bonobos, cofounders Spaly and Dunn grabbed attention by differentiating the product. Available in distinctive and uniquely named colors (Mint Julep, Pink Party Starters, and Panta Claus, a.k.a. red plaid), Bonobos's clothes stood out in a crowd. Word spread quickly among Spaly's and Dunn's fellow students at Stanford's business school—giving them a jump-start on sales. The notion that comfort and style could be achieved with minimal annoyance merely by logging on to a website and clicking on a few measurements was salient to Bonobos's targeted market of busy young professionals.

Starbucks Regrabbing Attention

Even before the 2008 economic downturn, Starbucks' performance was suffering, as evidenced by a 40 percent decline in stock prices from February 2007 to February 2008. Customer loyalty was evaporating, and the firm was forced to close six hundred of its seventeen thousand stores in 2008 and three hundred more in 2009. After years of explosive growth, Starbucks faced a number of significant brand challenges.

Loss of the perception of its exclusivity and quality. Having previously billed itself as the "third place" outside of home and work, Starbucks was now on every corner.

Loss of sense of intimacy with customers and communities. In February 2007, a leaked internal memo written by founder Howard Schultz noted, "Stores no longer have the soul of the past and reflect a chain of stores vs. the warm feeling of a neighborhood store."[6]

Loss of trust. As Starbucks became a global megabrand akin to Walmart, it began to suffer from the general crisis of trust in the good faith of corporate USA.[7]

Starbucks knew it needed not only to change direction but also to grab the attention of a jaded world. To start, it launched a fair trade campaign and became the world's largest buyer of fair trade certified coffee, aiming to offer coffee farmers in Latin America and East Africa more rewarding opportunities.[8] Starbucks also introduced the world's first coffee cup made of 10 percent recycled materials, and the company is working with suppliers to develop 100 percent recyclable paper coffee cups.[9]

Starbucks went to the Web and became an avid Twitter user, created a blog, and created a My Starbucks Idea page powered by Salesforce CRM ideas functionality. Each of these three social media channels helps Starbucks interact with customers in a unique way. Twitter allows the company to send quick messages to customers. The Starbucks Ideas in Action blog and the My Starbucks Idea website take it to another level, allowing the firm to engage with its customers, and integrate and manage feedback.

Starbucks effectively grabbed the attention of the world with its socially responsible agenda. A 2010 Web search on "Starbucks" and "fair trade" yielded more than 442,000 results, including mentions in every major media outlet as well as specialty publications—both online and offline—and thousands of blogs.

How do you grab attention? Again, we look to design thinking for guidance. In the first wing, Focus, you began to develop a deep understanding of the state of mind and attitude of your audience. What would turn their heads? By rapidly prototyping your ideas—testing several concepts on your audience to see what sticks—you can come up with the best way to grab their attention appropriately.

Next, we'll discuss four key design principles that will help you hook your user, and then turn to metrics so you can get a sense of how to prototype and test your ideas.

Design Principles to Grab Attention

Design Principle 1: Get Personal

You turn and look when someone calls your name. Why? Messages that metaphorically call out your name cultivate feelings of personal relevance. And that is more likely to lead to engagement and behavior change. What is the metaphorical equivalent of calling someone's name with social media? Tagging is one mechanism. Take the campaign that the Gift of Life donor program, an East Coast–based organ and tissue donor program, used to promote its Facebook page. The organization had a camera crew of volunteers and staffers at its big annual fundraiser, the Dash for Organ & Tissue Donor Awareness. They took photos of supporters holding signs with facts about their organization and organ donation. The crew then gave each person a sticker with information about how to find the photos on Facebook. Participants went to Facebook, became fans of the page, and tagged themselves in the photos. Every photo they tagged appeared in their news feed, which would be seen by all their friends, people who presumably would share similar interests. It worked incredibly fast: page views jumped from 11 to 800 overnight.

Facebook is a powerful medium for fostering—and continuing—a personal connection. One organization that does this particularly well is the Somaly Mam Foundation, a non-profit that helps survivors of sexual slavery. The organization, which supports rescue, shelter, and rehabilitation programs across Southeast Asia, where the trafficking of women and girls—some as young as five—is widespread practice, was founded by Somaly Mam, an activist and a survivor. Without Somaly, this cause could have been relegated to a faceless issue—one that feels distant, difficult to even imagine. However, through social media, Somaly, who lives in Cambodia, has reduced the distance (physical and otherwise) between her and the rest of the world. Through Facebook, Somaly interacts with individuals all over the world, responding to comments on the page and providing personal insights from the perspective of the girls in Cambodia. The personal interaction builds an emotional connection between Somaly and those who follow her work.

Note that eliciting emotion is vital to crafting personally relevant messages. Think of emotionally charged images that grab your attention—for example, any one of the images of the Twin Towers falling on 9/11. A large part of our response is due to our wiring. Brain-imaging studies reveal that when people are shown emotionally intense pictures, they are more stimulated than if shown emotionally neutral pictures,[10] and they spend more time looking at them.

Whether you're selling shoes or soliciting donations for your favorite nonprofit, employing visuals, words, or concepts that personally resonate with potential customers or contributors will make them care about your effort. One of the most universal "hooks" that resonates with people is the simple matter of how they spend their time. By referencing time, marketers have found that they can tap into more favorable attitudes—and sell more.[11]

We put this theory to the test with C&D's Lemonade Stand. With the able assistance of our sons, Cooper and Devon, we experimented with how to best engage customers using three different signs. The first sign read "Spend a little time and enjoy C&D's lemonade." The second read, "Spend a little money and enjoy C&D's lemonade." The third sign was neutral, simply saying, "Enjoy C&D's lemonade." Only one sign was displayed at a time, and customers were given the option of paying whatever they wanted for each glass of lemonade. When the first sign—the sign emphasizing time—was displayed, twice as many passersby noticed the stand and bought lemonade. They also paid twice as much as when the money sign was displayed. Simple and subtle rewording led to more people stopping and looking, twice the conversion rate at twice the average price, yielding four times the revenue.

One of our favorite real-world examples of the power of the Time-Ask Effect comes from the software industry's Mozilla Foundation, a community built almost entirely around donated time.[12] Dedicated to the idea that the Internet is a public resource, Mozilla uses a collaborative and transparent process to nurture a global community of volunteer developers who build and enhance open-source products, such as the Firefox browser and the Thunderbird email client. They don't ask for money as much as they ask for time. Mozilla's invitations to join the community and donate time catch people's attention and feel more personal; volunteers and employees consistently talk about the degree to which Mozilla speaks to them—uniquely. The concept of personal time investment has yielded a community of deeply loyal users. In addition, the Firefox browser is widely considered to be more secure and have fewer bugs than the Microsoft product—a fact that is largely credited to the dedication of its huge network of professional and amateur testers, who pore over the computer code to detect and address problems.

Design Principle 2: Deliver the Unexpected

In an overmessaged world with overwhelmed subjects, your message must surprise. So why are so many of the techniques used by marketers, by definition, formulaic? Too often strategies and tactics are mimicked in a predictable way. Such retread strategies are more likely to fail. Something is new and original, and thus attention getting, only the *first* time you hear it. Why only the first time? Because humans are biologically wired to be attuned to surprise. Researchers such as Emmanuel Donchin have identified a brain-wave pattern called P300 that occurs when the human brain notices something surprising or something that grabs attention.[13]

Grabbing Your Attention Immediately

Lead with what is important to the audience. Famed talk-show host Oprah Winfrey suggests that you ask yourself, "What's the most important message you want to leave your audience with—*and why should they care*? Every listener instinctively wants to know one thing: What's in it for me? The greatest public speakers are those who work at making their addresses both interesting and *relatable*."[14]

Start with a fact. Grab attention with a simple, striking statistic or factual statement: a market growth figure or a detail about an economic, demographic, or social trend with which your audience may not be familiar. The more surprising the fact, the better.

Begin with a question. Open-ended questions command an audience's attention and pique their curiosity. However, the question needs to be intriguing and easily woven into your presentation's theme. Continue on this path by making the subsequent message interactive. Have audience members do something (for example, take off their shoes, pull out their cell phones to discuss how a company is making the small chips inside, tweet a message). Such invitations to interact break the ice and allow for further conversation.

Employ humor, but strategically and carefully. Many believe that humor comes in one shape and size, and wonder whether or not they should attempt it. However, there are many types of humor—sarcastic, deadpan, silly, clever. Just think of Ellen DeGeneres ("laugh at life") versus Chris Farley ("laugh at me") versus Andrew Dice Clay ("laugh at others"). Because the main risk is turning off your audience, choose carefully based on whom you are trying to reach.

The element of surprise in marketing has been particularly effective in influencing viral behavior. In a study that analyzed successful and global viral marketing campaigns, researchers discovered that surprise was the dominant emotion identified by consumers within each campaign.[15]

You need to be original to grab attention. As Seth Godin, author of *Purple Cow: Transform Your Business by Being Remarkable,* argues: "The leader is the leader precisely because he did something remarkable. And once that remarkable thing is taken—it's no longer remarkable when *you* decide to do it. . . . You can't be remarkable by following someone else who's remarkable."[16] You need to develop a metaphorical purple cow, a cow that looks different enough from all the other cows in the pasture to surprise passersby lulled by the sameness of black and white. Think of what differentiates Sam Adams beer from Budweiser, or Yamaha (electric keyboards) from conventional pianos. Further, Godin layers on a need to focus on distinctive "original" niche audiences. "The old rule was this: Create safe products and combine them with great marketing. Average products for average people. *That's broken.* The new rule is: Create remarkable products that the right people seek out."[17] Bob Sutton, author of *Weird Ideas That Work,* argues that one mechanism is simply to reverse the rules; observe what others do—and then do the opposite.

Consider Coke. In 2009 the company was looking for a new way to connect to young consumers. Spending on traditional media or Super Bowl ads would be predictable. Instead they veered far from what could have been anticipated and delivered "The Happiness Machine." Just before final exams, Coke installed a vending machine in a university cafeteria, but instead of dispensing normal sodas, the machine dispensed unexpected surprises. When a student paid for one Coke, she got many Cokes . . . and then got other treats as well: flowers, a pizza, balloon animals, and even a ten-foot-long sandwich.

The students in the cafeteria were delighted by the surprises, and as they shared the treats with fellow students, the good will was tangible. Coke posted a video on YouTube and advertised it with a single tweet ("Would you like a Coca-Cola Happiness Machine? Share the happiness . . . share the video. http://CokeURL.com/HappinesMachine"). Within two weeks, the video had been watched 2 million times. Although traditional Coke ads, such as those placed on *American Idol*, would reach a larger audience, Coke's initial data suggest that the Happiness Machine has had a much more meaningful impact with consumers. Coke spent less than $50,000 on the video and proved the power of surprise as a tool to establishing a deep emotional connection.[18] One student responded, "I want to give it a hug!" In the words of another: "Thank you Coke."

Design Principle 3: Visualize Your Message

Show, don't tell. Don't underestimate the importance of your visual identity. As a species, we remember 85 to 90 percent of what we see, but less than 15 percent of what we hear.[19]

When it comes to social judgments, physical characteristics often determine whether we notice—and they shape our impressions.[20] Baby-faced people are thought of as honest, warm, and more approachable.[21] People with masculine features (large jaws, prominent brow ridges) are perceived to be more dominant.[22] What is your product or campaign's "physical appearance"? Consider Apple's white iPod earbuds. Prior to the iPod, nearly all earbuds were black. White earbuds not only made the iPod stand out but also may have helped create a perception that more individuals owned iPods than actually did, as distinctiveness can create the impression that something is bigger than it is[23] or more widely adopted than it is.[24] And if the friends and acquaintances of iPod's target customer all appeared to have invested in iPods, that consumer might think it worth considering as well, or so Apple designers hoped.

One example of a campaign that successfully relies on visual images to conjure up a spectrum of strong emotions is Rock the Vote, whose mission is to engage and build the political power of young people in order to spark progressive change. Rock the Vote had been around since 1992, but didn't achieve explosive growth until social media offered it a means of direct communication with college-age unregistered voters. In its initial year, it registered 350,000 young people; in 2008, by leveraging an online, mobile, and grassroots outreach, it massively grew that number to more than 2.6 million.

Just how did Rock the Vote do it? The organizers created a viral campaign by utilizing graphic (fear-based) images to portray such issues as rape, abortion, gun control, and capital punishment. The goal: to grab attention and shock youth into voting. The campaign has achieved staggering results, including running the largest youth voter registration drive in history in 2008. The organization's volunteers, staff, and partners crossed the country (sixteen states, twenty-three artists, one hundred stops, fifteen thousand miles) in colorful buses to promote voter registration, education, early voting, and action. Some 251,000 voters signed up for its mobile activist list, 1.6 million joined its email list, and 5.7 million visited its website.

The impact? Some 22 million eighteen- to twenty-nine-year-olds—more than ever before in U.S. history—voted in 2008.[25]

Or consider Nike, who partnered with (RED) to launch the (RED) laces campaign on World AIDS day. Nike created eye-catching (RED) shoelaces, donating 100 percent of the sale proceeds to fight AIDS. Working with Twitter, the company came up with creative ways to promote the movement, including turning red the text of all tweets that included the hashtag #red or #laceupsavelives. To ignite the Twitter community, Nike enlisted social influencers—including Serena Williams, John Legend, Ashton Kutcher, and Chris Rock, among others—to tweet or retweet an item with those hashtags. Within one day, they reached over ten million people with their message, turned more than half a million tweets red through the use of the promotion's hashtags, and made Worlds AIDS day a top five global trending topic on Twitter, driving sales of the (RED) laces and ensuring further reach well beyond the followers of a particular set of influencers.

Precisely because the advertising landscape is so cluttered and it's so difficult to grab anyone's attention, marketers have been playing with images to surprise, startle, and occasionally shock their audiences. This effort takes a number of different forms. For years, researchers have theorized that people interpret visual images in ways that transcend the literal picture.[26] This tendency of people to view images as symbolic was successfully exploited by an earlier series of Apple advertisements, Think Different, in which icons of artistic creativity and innovation—Albert Einstein, Joan Baez, and Pablo Picasso, among others—were meant to suggest that anyone who used Apple products would find themselves in the same illustrious company.

MasterCard's Priceless campaign does much the same, by presenting images of life experiences that money can't buy.

Researchers attempting to analyze the effectiveness of visual advertisements found that the visual techniques used fell into three categories. *Juxtaposition* consists of two different images next to each other, *fusion* combines two separate images, and *replacement* refers to using an image to evoke another image in the mind of the audience.[27] Replacement is the most complex and effective form of this visual shorthand, which is designed to grab attention and thus persuade. One classic replacement ad, used in the 1980s, depicted an ill-seeming, debauched-looking middle-aged man with the caption "Smoking is very glamorous." The absent image it was supposed to evoke, of course, was that of a beautiful young man or woman—the kind of man or woman typically found in a smoking advertisement.

The case for including images is compelling. In one study, D. L. Nelson showed that pictures and words hold different places in memory and that pictures trump words in terms of grabbing attention because they're composed of lines and curves that are more complex, and therefore distinctive, than the lines and curves that compose words.[28] Along similar lines, a study at the University of Pennsylvania showed that in presentations, when information is conveyed orally, people retain only 10 percent of the content. But when a presentation includes visuals and words, the number increases to 50 percent.[29]

All this demonstrates that attaching your message to powerful visual images gives your audience the ability to think in a deeper manner about your message, about how it relates to them personally. What visual images do you own?

> ## Table for Two: A Japanese Program to Fight Hunger and Obesity
>
> Table for Two is a Japan-based nonprofit that addresses famine in developing countries and simultaneously tackles obesity in developed countries. The organization sells healthy meals in corporate and school cafeterias and cafes and for each sale it donates twenty cents, the cost of a school meal, to buy a lunch for a child in Africa.
>
> Instead of pleading with people to give money to feed the hungry, Table for Two came up with a creative name and supported it with a compelling visual image. The logo is an image of two lunch tables (one full and one empty) abutted so as to form the shape of a T. This visual image serves to grab attention and differentiates Table for Two from other nonprofits with similar goals.

Design Principle 4: Make a Visceral Connection

Design your campaign with the primitive brain in mind. You're likely already familiar with the attention-grabbing power of sensory-based images.

A number of top brands have created marketing campaigns based on concepts that have evoked one or more of the senses, including Absolut Vodka, Starbucks, and the Four Seasons Hotel chain.[30] Just think about color: Lance Armstrong owns yellow; Coke owns red; Breast Cancer, pink. Each of these colors not only grabs your attention but makes your visual experience with the brand that much more memorable.

Scents also have a powerful role to play in grabbing attention. In one experiment, college students were asked to examine one of two types of brand-name pencils, one that was unscented or one that smelled like tea tree oil. Two weeks later, the average student could not remember a single attribute of the scentless pencil, but remembered more than three attributes of the scented pencils.[31]

Sound—and in particular music—is another critical tool. Although much has been said and done to tap the power of sound (think Intel chime) or music (think YouTube videos that you share with friends), less is known about *why* certain music grabs attention. Research from Stanford suggests that, surprisingly, it may not be the type of music you use for your campaign or brand that grabs attention, as much as it is the pace of the music and whether *changes* in music are worked in. The research team demonstrated that music engages the areas of the brain involved with paying attention, making predictions, and updating the event in memory.[32] Peak brain activity occurred during a short period of silence between musical

Four Design Principles to Grab Attention

PUVV

Personal. Create with a personal hook in mind.

Unexpected. People like consuming and then sharing new information. Draw them in by piquing their curiosity. Look to reframe the familiar.

Visual. Show, don't tell. Photos and videos speak millions of words. Synthesize your thoughts with quick visuals.

Visceral. Design your campaign so that it triggers the senses: sight, sound, hearing, or taste. Use music to tap into deep, underlying emotions.

movements when seemingly nothing was happening. When the expected progression of music doesn't occur—that's when the brain starts paying attention. So don't just include sound and music—consider how you are using those tools to make a visceral connection.

Ideate, Prototype, Test— Measure, Measure, Measure

You'll need to gauge the effectiveness of every presentation or campaign, and that means you'll need to measure how well you're grabbing the attention of your audience. For each effort, the metrics might be different, and you'll need to monitor several metrics. These might include the number of unique visitors, the number of sign-ups, the amount of money lent or donated, the amount of time spent on the home page (if online), and the number of times the message is forwarded (if electronic) or mentioned.

It's important to map out those metrics before you launch your effort, and to check in and evaluate your progress toward meeting your goals and metrics. Establishing a baseline gives you something against which to measure progress and should coincide with your goals.

Google and Twitter help you track the online elements of your campaign. Google Analytics allows you to see the number of users who visit your site and to measure the engagement of your audience and power of your appeal by tracking the amount of time users spend on your Web page, as well as visitor bounce rate.

Similarly, Twitter @ mentions (@yourtwitterusername) allow you to track the attention of your audience (at least on

Twitter). An @ mention is a public reply to something you said, or a mention of you in some other context. In general, more of these is better than fewer, and you can benchmark yourself against others with this metric. Number of followers is another metric, but like page views on a website, that measurement can be misleading. It's much more important to have 1,000 "quality" followers than 10,000 "low-quality" followers. (The difference is that one set is made up of engaged people reading your tweets, and the other may be comprised of abandoned accounts and spam bots.) Because the way many people build large follower numbers is by auto-following anyone who follows them, a mark of low quality or of your own low quality to someone else is a high following-to-follower ratio. A ratio higher than 0.5:1 is generally not good once you get into the several hundreds or thousands of people. It's simply impossible to actually listen to several thousand twitterers.

You can evaluate your campaign's ability to grab attention by determining whether it serves as a social media tipping point. To do that, you need to determine whether your campaign has set off a chain reaction, a process by which something becomes viral on the whole social Web. The "social media tipping points and chain reactions" metric determines whether your idea finds its way to a preexisting forum that could spread your idea. Possible questions to ask are: Did my idea or message make the front page of Digg.com? Is it a trending topic on Twitter? Is it a top video on YouTube? If you can answer yes to at least one of these questions, congrats! You've reached a tipping point and have a shot at setting off a chain reaction. The next step is determining how to keep this momentum going and your audience engaged.

Getting Started with Twitter

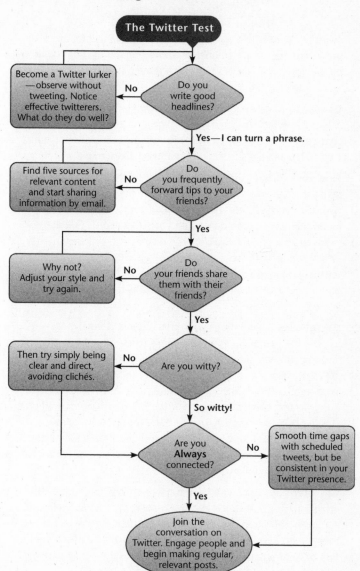

The Twitter Test

Do you write good headlines?

No → Become a Twitter lurker —observe without tweeting. Notice effective twitterers. What do they do well?

Yes—I can turn a phrase.

Do you frequently forward tips to your friends?

No → Find five sources for relevant content and start sharing information by email.

Yes

Do your friends share them with their friends?

No → Why not? Adjust your style and try again.

Yes

Are you witty?

No → Then try simply being clear and direct, avoiding clichés.

So witty!

Are you **Always** connected?

No → Smooth time gaps with scheduled tweets, but be consistent in your Twitter presence.

Yes

Join the conversation on Twitter. Engage people and begin making regular, relevant posts.

Twitter Boot Camp

Twitter is a microblogging platform that enables its users to publish (or "tweet") their answer to the simple question "What's happening?" The catch is that the answer has to be 140 characters or fewer.

Get started. Make sure your Twitter profile is interesting and, if possible, witty. Upload a fun background and a good picture, something that is easily identifiable and that draws attention. Include a link to your site so that people can learn more.

Find your target market. Once you're ready, start using Twitter's search, http://search.twitter.com, to find others who have tweeted about subjects related to your cause. Think about people in the news, brand names, and other keywords that are relevant to your project. Evaluate the results, and choose whether or not to follow those users. Also consider looking at their followers, who might share similar interests and could either be in your target market or have large networks that could help you spread the word.

Get followers. Remember, your goal is to get as many followers as possible (generally speaking, more followers = more traffic) and to get the "highest-quality" (influential and relevant) followers as possible. Once a day, spend thirty minutes working your Twitter follow list. At the risk of recanting what we've said earlier, but with the understanding that this is a good method when starting out, the simplest way to get a lot of initial followers is simply to follow a lot of people. A lot of people will follow anyone who follows them, so this basically means that by following them you gain a follower.

Get attention. Once you have followers, how do you get their attention? The best way is via an @ reply that contains a relevant comment, question, or piece of information for them. Follow their tweets live and all the time. Sometimes they'll post a question or a comment, and when you can add value, reply to them using the @ reply. See http://dragonflyeffect.com.

Tweet smart. Try to keep your tweets different and fresh. Don't just blast links to your website with little to no context—that's spamlike, and people hate it. Mix things up. Send pictures out via twitpic; people always love pictures. Post a daily question or a caption. Create a contest: tweet the question of the day and include a link, making people want to participate. Then close the loop by tweeting the top response and linking to the other top responses. Last, good articles that you run across (or retweet from someone else) are always appreciated—in moderation and with the right context.

WING 3
Engage

How to Make People Connect with Your Goal

> *To succeed you need to find something to hold on to,*
> *something to motivate you, something to inspire you.*
> —TONY DORSETT

Ami Adjaho, an entrepreneur in Togo, a small agriculture-dependent country in West Africa, needed a $675 loan to expand her business, which sold charcoal and yams in her village. Daariimaa, thirty-nine, who lived with her aunt and two sons in a traditional nomadic tent in the Uvurkhangai province of Mongolia, wanted a $2,975 loan to purchase fabric and tools to grow her well-respected dressmaking business. And Malamine Diallo, a twenty-seven-year-old entrepreneur who lived with his extended family in a working-class suburb in the Republic of Mali, sought a $1,150 loan to expand his store, which sold food, toiletries, and mobile phone cards to neighborhood families.

Just a few years ago it would have been nearly impossible for Adjaho, Daariimaa, and Diallo to get any sort of loan to grow their businesses. Today they are just three of the thousands of globally far-flung entrepreneurs who have received the funding they need to thrive. The money didn't come from local lenders, global banks, or aid organizations; it came from people like us . . . people like you.

Perhaps you are familiar with the nonprofit Kiva (www .kiva.org), one of the world's first person-to-person microlending enterprises. On its website, Kiva posts loan requests from entrepreneurs in some of the world's poorest nations. Anyone can sign up, choose an entrepreneur, and become a lender, fighting the cycle of poverty by helping people help themselves. In 2005, its first year, Kiva distributed more than $500,000 to entrepreneurs. The funds were mostly sourced from individuals in increments of just $25. In its second year, Kiva loaned more than $14 million; in its third, nearly $50 million. Since Kiva's inception, more than 631,345 people have loaned over $111 million.

The numbers are impressive, but Kiva is about much more than that. It's about replacing daunting statistics on global poverty with compelling individual stories, and enabling personal connections. Kiva's cofounders, Jessica Jackley, who in 2005 was working in rural Kenya, Tanzania, and Uganda with Village Enterprise Fund, and Matt Flannery, then a software developer at TiVo, were well aware of poverty's toll on individuals and families. When developing their plan for Kiva, they decided to avoid taking a conventional aid-organization approach to marketing. They wanted to cut through the abstraction of poverty, and, drawing on Jessica's experience in the field, they focused on telling stories about entrepreneurs like Adjaho, who is now able to provide ample fuel and food to her fellow villagers, and Diallo, who in growing his store improved his life and the lives of those around him.

Through these stories, Kiva established a bond between lenders and entrepreneurs that proved incredibly powerful: in four years, Kiva has made a difference in the lives of 217,000 entrepreneurs in forty-nine countries. Not only have entrepreneurs received loans, but they've kept their commitment to lenders: Kiva boasts a 98 percent repayment rate.[1]

Along the way, Kiva itself became a story people love to tell. President Bill Clinton wrote about Kiva in his book *Giving*. *New York Times* journalist Nicholas Kristof described his experience with Kiva in an editorial, which became the third most forwarded article on nytimes.com the day it appeared. Within three days, his readers had loaned over $250,000. Later, when Oprah Winfrey featured Kiva on her television show, the surge of visitors following the broadcast crashed Kiva's site for four days.

If Grab Attention is about getting people to notice your cause, Engage is about what happens next—compelling people to care deeply, maybe even fall in love. Engage is arguably the most challenging of the four wings, because love occurs infrequently, and engaging others is more of an art than a science. Engagement has little to do with logic or reason. You might have brilliant arguments as to why people should get involved, but if you can't engage them emotionally, they won't be swayed.

As Kiva learned after the Oprah broadcast, media tends to amplify emotional appeal (or lack thereof). Take, for example, the televised debate between Richard Nixon and John F. Kennedy, which was widely credited with JFK's election. Voters gained access to something pivotal they could not discern by listening to the radio or reading the paper: the emotional tenor of the candidates. Nixon looked nervous; Kennedy looked energetic and statesmanlike. Social media has made it even simpler to amplify the message.

How to Engage Your Audience Through Social Media

For-profit companies have become increasingly savvy about engaging their customers through social media. As we've explored in Wing 2: Grab Attention, many have fan pages on Facebook or talk to their followers on Twitter. "Ideas" pages, like Starbucks' mystarbucksidea.com, allow companies to ask their customers directly what matters most to them. But not all companies are successful in their attempts to engage customers through social media. Here we'll explore several cases that illustrate what sets apart the campaigns that succeed.

In 2000—making it a classic story in the world of new media—Procter & Gamble's Pampers brand initiated one of the first and most authentic examples of engagement marketing. Pampers could have stuck to pedantically posting product-related information about diapers and potty-training on its website. Instead, marketers considered their customers: who they were, what they were going through, and what they needed most. The marketers found that a substantial portion of

Pampers buyers are first-time parents, who are inexperienced, confused, and tired. Pampers took this knowledge, found a fit with its familiar, trusted brand, and followed up with a Web strategy that transformed the Pampers website from a presentation of static brand information to a complete "new mom information portal." The site includes expert advice and articles covering the first few years of a child's life—from medical concerns to developmental issues to parenting best practices. Despite the fact that Pampers' website relaunch occurred at a time when store brands were undercutting Pampers' prices, Pampers sales rose from $718 million in 2001 to $826 million in 2006, and other major brands subsequently spent millions of dollars trying to emulate the brand's success.[2]

In another effective corporate example, in 2005, TV Guide.com relaunched its website with an invitation for users to participate. Eighteen months later, more than 10 percent of all the traffic was coming to see the user-generated content rather than the professionally generated content. In the same period, TVGuide.com's traffic increased 83 percent over the prior year.[3] TVGuide.com also implemented a search function that allowed visitors to search for specific topics or actors, increasing its stickiness and helping boost advertising revenues by 40 percent in the first year.[4]

Dell also found a way to engage with its audience—and boost sales—by building an online community around Dell Outlet, the computer maker's source for refurbished Dell products. In June 2007, Dell established the Twitter account @Dell Outlet and invited over one hundred employees at Dell to tweet to customers from handles such as @stephanieatdell or @lionel atdell. By April 2010, @DellOutlet attracted over 1.5 million followers, and ranked among the top 100 most followed Twitter accounts.[5] What fueled this growth? Twitter enabled Dell to instantly and directly send offers to an opt-in audience of followers. Consumers were able to complete a sale within minutes and they appreciated the easier way to communicate and find the products they coveted at a discount. Revenue from @DellOutlet has grown to over $3 million in the United States. Globally, Dell has garnered over $6.5 million in revenue from Twitter followers.[6]

Not only have corporations and nonprofits embraced social media, but the military has also found it to be a powerful tool in its arsenal. On July 8, 2009, a crew member of the USS *Shiloh* fell overboard as the Navy ship steamed toward the port of Yokosuka, Japan. Although the crew did everything they could, they couldn't retrieve the sailor from the ocean, and were forced to proceed to the port—where dozens of friends and family members were waiting to greet the crew after several weeks at sea.

When tragedies such as this occur, the Navy follows aggressive communication protocols. Within one hour of an incident, a statement should be released to the media to ensure that local communities are informed of anything that affects them. But Commander Jeff Davis, the fleet public affairs officer for the U.S. 7th Fleet, realized that a press release would not reach the family and friends waiting on the Yokosuka pier in time. Prior to the official press release, Commander Davis decided to inform the public of the tragedy via the U.S. 7th Fleet's Facebook page. Within minutes the news had swept the pier, and over the next few difficult hours, the 7th Fleet continuously updated the public without compromising professionalism or traditional family notification procedures. Over the next few days, the 7th Fleet's Facebook page became a forum for the missing sailor's friends, crew members, and well-wishers around the globe to share feelings, messages, and condolences.

In the midst of this tragedy, Commander Davis and his team achieved a significant goal: to be the preferred source of information about the fleet. They had learned from experience what would happen if they didn't take control and engage the military community: others would fill the void. For example, in 2007, a site called yokosukabase.com was created by an individual not officially affiliated with the Navy base to help U.S. families with the transition to the Yokosuka area. Today that site is still the preferred source of information about the base—much more popular among relocating Navy families than the official site of Naval Base Yokosuka. When Commander Davis arrived at the 7th Fleet, he wanted to ensure that this wouldn't happen to the fleet. In 2008, he set up accounts with Facebook, Flickr, MySpace, Twitter, and YouTube, and he has been carefully feeding and monitoring them ever since.

As of April 2010, the U.S. 7th Fleet had more than 6,000 fans on Facebook. "One of the fleet's persistent priorities is to build partnerships, and that requires us to promote transparency and foster goodwill," says Vice Admiral John Bird, 7th Fleet commander. "Social media has dramatically increased our ability to engage with people and tell them not only that we are here, but also to show them why we are here, and how our presence promotes regional stability, enables prosperity and fosters cooperative security."[7]

Characteristics of Highly Engaging Campaigns

Transparency. The brand shares news as it happens, even if it might not appear to be in its best interest. Example: Doctors Without Borders received so many responses to its request for funds to help the victims of the 2004 Indonesian tsunami that it quickly fulfilled its requirements. Rather than continuing to take donations for that cause and using them for some other purpose, the organization said that it could not ethically continue to accept donations for tsunami victims.

Interactivity. Information flows between community and brand, and actions are initiated by both producers and consumers. Example: VolunteerMatch has become the web's most popular volunteering network by designing a service that focuses on making it easier for good people and good causes to interact and take action.

Immediacy. The company releases information to the community as it becomes available, rather than waiting for discrete events, such as press releases, analyst calls, or quarterly reports. Example: When criticism started circulating in the press about Kiva, suggesting that it did not work the way the founders claimed, the company quickly dispelled misunderstanding on the Kiva blog.

Facilitation. The company acts as a caretaker of brand development rather than attempting to control it. Example: Kiva sends Kiva Fellows out into the field to find and promote stories of entrepreneurs, developing and augmenting the brand, without Kiva headquarters exerting control over the end result.

Commitment. The consumers of a product or service are as committed to its success as the producers or organizers are. Example: Ordinary people are both the consumers and contributors to the global reference site Wikipedia. In 2009, for the first time, its founder called upon the users of the ad-free site to contribute. The site raised $7.5 million that year.

Cocreation. Ideas and the implementation of those ideas are as likely to come from the community as from the brand itself. Example: A grassroots initiative started by eBay employees turned into the eBay Green Team, a global effort by buyers, sellers, and the company itself to promote greener consumer practices.[8]

Collaboration. Producers and consumers work hand in hand to develop the brand and achieve a goal. Example: Dell's IdeaStorm website allows customers to post their ideas about products Dell should introduce and to vote for the best ideas—and to become part of the product development process.

Experience. The consumers and company view its products or services as experiences, not just purchases. Example: When enthusiasts created the TiVo Community Forum online not long after TiVo's launch in 1999, TiVo wisely didn't move to stop it. Instead, TiVo allowed some of its employees to participate in the forum to help people get the most out of their experience.

Trust. As a result of transparency, cocreation, and collaboration, trust is built between the producers and the consumers of products and services. Example: Ben and Jerry's has earned trust by making the first climate-neutral ice cream, reflecting the values of its customers.

Four Design Principles of Engagement

To engage, it's necessary to view yourself (and your effort) as a brand. Although brand is *conveyed* by products, advertising, visual shortcuts, and people, what matters is the experience that it offers—and the emotional attachment people form as a result. A simple and apt definition of a brand is a *reputation*, based on a collection of memories. Here we will reveal how to use the four design principles of engagement to seed powerful, lasting memories.

Design Principle 1: Tell a Story

Stories move us, make us feel alive, and inspire us. As famed screenwriting coach (and author of the screenwriting bible, *Story*) Robert McKee says, "Story is not only our most prolific art form, but rivals all activities—work, play, eating, and exercise—for our waking hours. We tell and take in stories as much as we sleep—and even when we dream."[9]

Our appetite for stories reflects the basic human need to understand patterns of life—and not merely as an intellectual exercise. Alexander Steele, in *Writing Fiction,* argues that we need stories just as we need food. "Our curiosity, and perhaps insecurity, compels us to continually explore the who, what, where, when, and why of our existence."[10] And surprisingly, how we tell stories about our lives and relationships shapes our lives a great deal.[11]

Despite our love for stories, and the ease with which we tell them and criticize them (we are very quick to judge the plot of a movie, for example), most of don't think of ourselves as storytellers. How many of us put any thought into *how* stories are made? How many of us see the benefit of stories beyond entertainment? How can we harness the energy of a story?

The vast majority of us attempt to persuade using only the left side of the brain, which is to say, with logic and reason. Persuasion, though, occurs as much, if not more, through emotion. Indeed, writes Daniel Pink, author of *Drive,* "Right-brain dominance is the new source of competitive advantage."[12] By developing the right side of the brain, you can build engagement through "uniting an idea with an emotion."[13] Compelling stories do just that.

According to cognitive psychologist Roger Schank, humans aren't actually wired to understand logic; they're wired to grasp

How to Tell a Story

By **Oren Jacob**, *chief technical officer at Pixar Animation Studios and* **Justine Jacob**, *independent filmmaker*

- **Think arcs.** Story structure is critical because events need to build, one after the other, throughout your story. The pattern your story should follow is one of increasing risk and increasing consequences until the one final, inevitable conclusion occurs, but not in the way the audience expects it to.

- **Start wide.** Cull many stories, boil them down to their essence (the parts that reveal the most important aspects of each character), and then cut, cut, cut. Don't bore your audience with stuff they already know, or stuff they don't need to know. Give them just what they need, maybe a little bit less, and nothing else.

- **Know when to shut up.** Don't explain everything. Audiences are smarter than you are; let them draw their own conclusions and make their own interpretations. Efficient storytelling demonstrates respect for your audience.

stories. Barack Obama understood the important role storytelling would play in his campaign for the presidency. In March 2007, Sam Graham-Felsen, a writer and documentary filmmaker, was hired to tell stories and blog as part of the campaign's communications mission. Graham-Felsen said that his boss, Joe Rospars, told him he "wanted someone with a writing background to tell the story of how the Obama campaign was bigger than just Obama, how it was a movement of ordinary people around the country who wanted to get involved in the campaign, and how many of these people had never been active in a political campaign before."[14] In other words, stories were important in the 2008 election, but the most important stories were not about Obama; they were about his supporters.

In an effort to find these stories, Graham-Felsen spent the first several months of the campaign calling supporters and finding out who they were, the nature of their struggles, and what they were hoping Obama would do if elected. The campaign wove many of these stories into campaign materials, from emails to videos. "I think those profiles really helped shape the narrative that this was a bottom-up, grassroots effort," said Graham-Felsen. "We didn't want to do what a lot of other campaigns do, which is to regurgitate press releases. Instead of repeating what's in the news, we wanted to report what wasn't in the news—things that were happening at the grassroots level across the country."

Another storyteller, Kate Albright-Hanna, joined the Obama campaign as director of video to capture these moving stories on video and share them online. "Everything we did we carried in our hearts, and I think that's different than being a political operative, where you have focus groups and try to figure out how to target certain people," she said. "We approached it like we were part of a movement. I think a lot of other campaigns have missed opportunities where they think of the Internet as just another place to put their TV ads."

Most companies don't place a high value on stories. And yet the stories told by employees and by customers are significant assets. When brands realize that storytelling can enhance loyalty, advocacy, and hiring and retention, they start looking for stories everywhere, updating their websites with "tell us your story" pages and asking consumers and employees to post testimonials on YouTube. These efforts can yield hundreds, if not thousands, of stories. But once you've got them, where do you put them?

Storytelling Boot Camp

So how does one tell a good story? Would-be writers spend decades struggling with this. Here's your cheat sheet.

Keep your audience wondering what happens next. According to novelist E. M. Forster, "[A story] can only have one merit: that of making the audience want to know what happens next. And conversely, it can only have one fault: that of making the audience *not* want to know what happens next."[15]

Get attention fast. One way to do so is to begin the story *where the audience is*. According to the nationally recognized storytelling author, speaker, and consultant Andy Goodman, "This is your story's 'hook'—the description of a place, circumstance, or premise that everyone understands and with which they readily identify."[16]

Make it sticky. Draw your reader deeper through suspense, by providing partial information: giving the audience a taste of what's to come—but not giving them too much information. As they wonder what happens next, they become more engaged and the story becomes sticky in a way that makes it difficult for them to disengage.

Focus on the protagonist. It's important to personalize the protagonist, make the protagonist seem real so that the audience begins to feel a personal stake in what happens.

Home in on the protagonist's problems or barriers to achieving his goal. Ask yourself what the protagonist desires that he isn't getting. What is standing in his way?[17]

What do you want your audience to do? You might need to identify the kind of action you want the audience to take, or identify how they can help. By the end of your story, the audience should feel compelled to help or to take action.

The answer is a *storybank,* or a central online repository where you can easily and quickly find a story that enlivens whatever point you want to make. Andy Goodman argues this best: "Stories can be a powerful tool, but they can't help you if you can't find them when you need them."[18]

A particularly good example that highlights the power of video storybanking is the Kahani Movement (*kahani* means "story" in Hindi), a social network that challenges its members to collect stories from the first major wave of South Asians who emigrated to the United States, and to post this content to the Kahani website as well as to Facebook and Twitter.

Founded by brothers Dr. Sanjay Gupta of CNN and Suneel Gupta of Groupon, Kahani brings a traditional passion for storytelling into the Web 2.0 world. Interviews can be conducted in living rooms by anyone with a camera and an Internet connection. The stories people share are captivating because they are personal, accessible, and surprising. Take Suneel Gupta's own story:

> In 1968, in Ann Arbor, Michigan, my mom's car broke down. She was new to the area, having recently immigrated from India, and decided to walk to a phone booth and look up the most common Indian name she could think of: "Patel." There were two listed—she picked the first. Only Mr. Patel wasn't home. His roommate, Mr. Gupta, answered the phone. That's how my parents met.

Within a few months of its launch, Kahani had over five hundred members actively gathering and posting stories to the site. Why the traction? The mission of Kahani is clear and time-sensitive. Its call-to-action video opens with the line, "Some stories are never told . . . because no one asks."

Getting Started with Storytelling

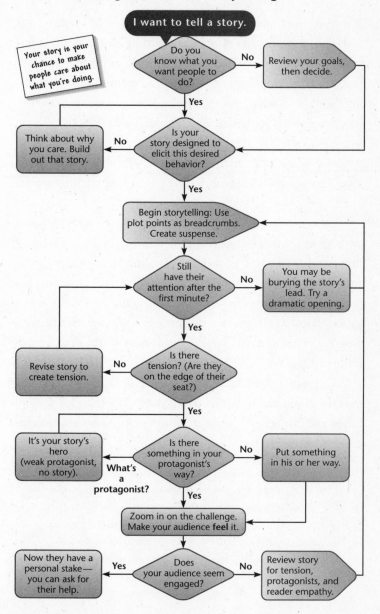

I want to tell a story.

Your story is your chance to make people care about what you're doing.

Do you know what you want people to do?

No → Review your goals, then decide.

Yes ↓

Is your story designed to elicit this desired behavior?

No → Think about why you care. Build out that story.

Yes ↓

Begin storytelling: Use plot points as breadcrumbs. Create suspense.

Still have their attention after the first minute?

No → You may be burying the story's lead. Try a dramatic opening.

Yes ↓

Is there tension? (Are they on the edge of their seat?)

No → Revise story to create tension.

Yes ↓

Is there something in your protagonist's way?

What's a protagonist?

It's your story's hero (weak protagonist, no story).

No → Put something in his or her way.

Yes ↓

Zoom in on the challenge. Make your audience **feel** it.

Does your audience seem engaged?

Yes → Now they have a personal stake—you can ask for their help.

No → Review story for tension, protagonists, and reader empathy.

Design Principle 2: Empathize

While you are starting a campaign intended to engage your audience, remember to first be engaged by them. What is important to them? How does that relate to your campaign? Have you created a campaign in which you can continuously (and easily) listen to your audience? Have you written words that resonate deeply with the reader? As Malcolm Gladwell noted, "Good writing does not succeed or fail on the strength of its ability to persuade. It succeeds or fails on the strength of its ability to engage you, to make you think, to give you a glimpse into someone else's head."[19]

We can become engaged with a brand—or with someone else's goals—for a broad range of reasons. Perhaps the most important is personal relevance. For example, if someone close to you is suffering from breast cancer, you might be more likely to give time or money to an organization that funds breast cancer research. If you are devoted to environmental causes, a brand that shows the same commitment could draw you in more easily.

Zappos's well-known CEO, Tony Hsieh, started tweeting in April 2007, and by April 2010 he had more than 1.7 million followers. His secret: thinking about his followers and brightening their day.

> When I first started using Twitter, I used to just tweet about what I was doing. Most of my tweets were very me-focused, because the guideline Twitter gives is to answer the question 'What are you doing right now?'" says Hsieh. "But then, I started sharing an inspirational quote or funny story or link to an interesting article. What I found was that those types of tweets also garnered the most responses. So today, with most of my tweets I try to do at least one of the following: cause my followers to smile with

something funny; inspire my followers (for example, with an inspirational quote), or enrich my followers' perspectives (such as with a link to an interesting article).[20]

Hsieh's delivering happiness is essential to Zappos's business. Developing relationships mean people come back—and repeat customers account for 75 percent of purchases.

Apply Hsieh's insight to your own campaign. To engage with others, you must empathize with your audience's needs and feelings. One way of creating an instant connection is to stress similarities with your target. Research shows that perceptions of similarity can increase rapport. One study found that when solicitors announced "I'm a student, too" when asking for charitable contributions on a college campus, they received double the amount of donations. Compliments also establish rapport, even when they are not true. Research at the University of North Carolina at Chapel Hill found that made-up compliments had just as great an effect as genuine ones.[21] We don't suggest that you lie to people, though. In addition to being distasteful, inauthenticity tends to backfire.

One of the most effective ways to engage your audience is to invoke what sociologists would call behavioral expectations. Typically, what other people are doing can have an enormous impact on what we choose to do. There's social pressure to conform, if only to feel connected to others. And much of behavior is contagious—research has shown that everything from yawning to laughing is "catching."[22] Therefore, as you learn about your users' goals and needs, also get to know their social identity—who is important to them.

One example is the cards hotels place in guest bathrooms, reminding guests that reusing towels will conserve natural resources. According to Noah Goldstein, a psychologist at UCLA, most people would be more persuaded by the message that other guests are hanging up their towels to conserve water. In one study, Goldstein and his colleagues told hotel guests that 75 percent of people who stayed in their exact hotel rooms previously had reused their towels. Towel conservation skyrocketed—even when the similar social group was arbitrarily defined. A simple act of social comparison can trigger conformity—and thus get people to do what you want them to do.[23]

COOKPAD Empathizes with Its Users— and Gains Engagement

COOKPAD was launched as a user-generated recipe site in 1998. Its founder, Aki Sano, wanted to make people happier by promoting better cooking. He thought, Who can stay grumpy with a great meal in front of them? Cultlike followers soon frequented the site, but Sano never promoted COOKPAD, as the site couldn't afford additional servers to support a larger user base. At one point, he even hid the site from search engines to curtail growth.

Sano was a purist: he did not want anything on the site that did not serve the singular goal of making cooking enjoyable. After years of operation, he decided to accept advertising, but only after asking its users if doing so was acceptable. To Sano's surprise, many were supportive and welcomed the ads, as they allowed the site to say in business.

Along the way, COOKPAD implemented many counterintuitive measures with two goals in mind:

- Keep user experience simple.
- Maintain healthy communities.

For simplicity, COOKPAD eliminated features that catered to recipe viewers, such as discussion forums and Q&A pages. Instead, COOKPAD invested in improving the experience of the recipe creators, since their recipes would attract viewers.

COOKPAD adopted several measures to keep the community healthy and happy. As a user-generated content site, COOKPAD risked flame wars between short-fused users. Sano determined that the problem often arose from a mob mentality. He made it impossible to search recipes by popularity, so casual users would not find star recipe creators easily, and creators would not form cults of personality. Viewer comments on recipes were limited to only thirty characters, making it virtually impossible to communicate anything more complicated than liking or disliking a recipe. This protected the recipe creators from overwhelming feedback, and let discrete communities grow around each creator in a manageable way.

Now COOKPAD is Japan's largest online recipe site, used regularly by one in four Japanese women in their thirties. Some 640,000 recipes have been uploaded, attracting 400 million page views and 8 million unique users monthly, of which 4 million come to the site almost every day. In July 2009, the company went public on Japan's Mothers Exchange, the fastest growing market in Japan, and became the most successful technology IPO of the year.

Design Principle 3: Be Authentic

The poet Robert Frost said, "No tears in the writer, no tears in the reader." If you're not truly moved by the story you're telling, no one else will be, either. You can only engage your audience with something that engages you. The place to start is by seeking out what is real and personal *for you* about your particular cause. Understanding that will lead you to what might engage others.

Studies have demonstrated that anything that increases feelings of closeness and connection between individuals increases the lengths to which they will go to offer assistance. In one study, researchers asked individuals whether they would volunteer to work for a charity. The number of people who acquiesced doubled if they personally knew someone who would benefit from that charity.[24] Similarly, people tend to give more money to victims who are personally identified rather than anonymous, or victims represented by statistics.[25] Using images of victims is powerful when trying to reduce "social distance." (Charities know that emotion on a face matters, and that viewers donate more time and money when that emotion is sad, as opposed to happy or neutral.)[26]

So step out from the background, get ahead of the numbers, and put a name, face, and a few personal facts behind your cause, and you will see increased engagement. You can't stop with an introduction. You must remain in frequent and constant communication. The subject must be difficult, if not impossible, to ignore. The way to ensure that the cause becomes compelling and authentic to people is to incorporate a wide variety of details that may strike different chords in different people over time.

Although the basic premise that authenticity matters has always resonated, many have argued that authenticity is particularly important in this Web 2.0 world—partly because there are fewer artificial barriers standing between us. Ravi Dhar, professor at the Yale School of Management, and his coauthor, George Newman, have shown that the more authentic consumers perceive a brand to be, the more they value it.[27]

What types of brands are seen as authentic? Those that are seen as organic (for example, Etsy, COOKPAD), as consistent (for example, Coke, Apple), or as having a clear values-based mission (for example, Google's "Don't Be Evil").[28] Interestingly, though, whereas many brands believe that they are being authentic, consumers often disagree. Why is there often a gap

EXPERT INSIGHTS

The Corporate Social Networking Manifesto

*By **Loic Le Meur**, founder of Seesmic.com and LeWeb.net*

- **Show us real people.** In your videos and photos, use real people, not models or stock photography. Real people carry much more emotion.

- **Identify your best fans.** Find the people most committed to your company and make it easy for them to share information about your brand.

- **Love your users.** Give them small gifts and access to special events or products.

between a brand's beliefs about its authenticity and consumers' perceptions? One reason may be that authenticity comprises two factors: (1) having a strong values-based mission (Who are you, and why do you exist?) and (2) possessing the skills and ability to execute on that mission. Although companies are often privy to their own values-based mission, they don't always have the skills and abilities to execute on that vision. In other cases, perceptions of authenticity may suffer because the company simply doesn't tell its own story well, failing to convey its values-based mission. With social media, authenticity matters more than ever before.

Being authentic is as simple as being open, clear, and genuine. We look to Kiva as a prime example of how to do this well. Much of Kiva's success is due to its authenticity. Kiva's philosophy and culture were built on trust and what its founders call "radical transparency." The model is based on disseminating real information about the entrepreneurs—not marketing them. "The entrepreneurs on Kiva are not promotional material," says Jackley. "They are real people who have real challenges and dreams."[29]

Kiva's founders and staff are committed to sharing stories that earn respect instead of evoking pity. "When I see a picture of a woman on our site and it shows all the information about her, I begin to call her an entrepreneur," says Jackley. "She's not just a nameless face. She lives in a particular place. She has a business name. She has a nickname, Lizzie, and she needs $900. She has plans and a story." Since the founding of Kiva, it's been Jackley's goal to engage people by making them feel a positive emotional connection. She wanted to offer an alternative to what her generation had seen growing up—ads to alleviate poverty where "the message was to feel bad for these people and then to act."

Kiva's engagement strategy has never been to make you feel bad about the money you just spent on a double latte, which, if you were a good person, you would instead have used to feed a starving child in the developing world. Instead, Kiva introduces you to specific people whom you can help by loaning—not giving—money. The organization tells you exactly how the money will be spent, and you decide whom you'd like to invest in. If inspired, you can pick multiple entrepreneurs in different parts of the developing world to create a Kiva portfolio. Kiva's approach evokes the same thrill as planting a garden and then watching it grow, a process that both engages and inspires, which is part of what makes it sustainable.

Kiva strikes a fine balance between sharing compelling information and overwhelming potential lenders with too much information. Although nailing this balance might be nuanced, it can be learned.

"I think there's a sweet spot on Kiva where we have [just] enough information [so] that people can absorb it," said

Jackley. "We have the picture of the entrepreneur, the narrative, the bullet points such as name, location, business, amount, etc. Below that, as the story unfolds, we have bullet points of repayment on this date, and the journals. . . . There are some other websites that I think have too much information on them, and that can be really bad."

Kiva does a lot of listening to its constituents—a practice that was rooted in Jackley's "dream job" four years earlier, when she worked at the Village Enterprise Fund (VEF) in Africa. The VEF gave $100 grants to entrepreneurs to start or grow small businesses, and Jackley's job was to evaluate the impact of the money on the entrepreneurs' lives. She traveled from village to village interviewing grant and loan recipients and documenting their stories. Today, Kiva Fellows go out into the field to interview businesses, conduct "soft audits," and blog about what they see (since the best ideas are the easiest to replicate). Each Kiva Fellow is armed with a Flip video camera so that he or she can post videos of the interviews on the Kiva website. By 2009, about 20 percent of all Kiva entrepreneurs had been featured in these video and text blogs.

The storytelling doesn't stop with the recipients, however. Lenders are likewise encouraged to tell their stories, especially those about why they loan through Kiva. Along the way, they typically evangelize the businesses, people, and regions in which they've invested. Each lender has a personal portfolio page that displays whatever information he or she chooses to disclose—including name, age, location, photos, and reasons for lending, as well as information about the entrepreneurs he or she has funded. For example, Kari Dykes, a twenty-six-year-old Canadian marketing manager, regularly loans $25 to entrepreneurs across the world. Her pet projects have ranged from funding an ice-block seller in Togo, West Africa, to lending money to a barbecue-stand owner in Samoa. "It's amazing because I'm able to help people who have business ideas and want to grow," said Dykes in an article in the *Toronto Star.* "The loans help them jump the hurdle of having no capital."[30] Every entrepreneur Dykes has invested in thus far has paid her back within the agreed-on time period.

Lenders like Dykes are everyday people, not affluent donors or worldly philanthropists. Kiva has built a platform where they too come across as authentic, as people with whom other potential lenders can identify, making them part of Kiva's success in engaging its audience.

Video Boot Camp

Video-sharing sites such as YouTube or Vimeo are easy to sign up for, so your focus should be on creating good content that is well suited to video sharing (right quality, length, and so on) as well as to viewers and the situations in which they will see it. Think of an online video that you recently watched. Did you watch all the way to the end? Did you forward it? If a website was mentioned or linked, did you visit it? Here's what you'll need to consider to create videos that will be watched to the end— and passed on.

The shot. Rules of good photography apply: subjects looking at the camera or at the other people in the shot, good lighting, steady camera, no distracting backgrounds, and tight shots of people's faces. Take test shots; view them on your computer and make changes as necessary. Video tends to require more light than still photography. In the era of the iPhone and the Flip video camera, webcams are simply not good enough for your efforts; use them only if you have no alternative (and find an alternative quickly).

The cut. Anybody can make decent-quality video by using iMovie (Mac) or Windows Movie Maker (PC). Cut out garbage and add focus by inserting titles, images, or separate audio that supports your message. Avoid splashy transitions or effects—they are distracting and impress no one.

The subject. Focus on what you want to communicate. Work with a three-column script outlining (1) who is speaking, (2) what they are saying, and (3) what the picture is for each shot—it will help you focus on the elements you want to communicate. Make the most of sound and visuals. Memorize your script enough to get it right, while still coming across as authentic and engaging. (Be careful not to over-rehearse.) One of the most painful parts of this experience will be watching the first few takes, but you must. Pay particular attention to your word choices. Written English can sound stiff when spoken.

The analytics. YouTube features built-in analytics for every video, revealing the hot spots where people were most engaged, and also where they dropped off. You can also use these tools to compare similar appeals employing slightly differing creative content. Review these statistics as you plan subsequent videos.

The target. Although inroads have been made to get YouTube onto people's TVs, the majority of viewers will view your work on a computer or mobile device. Their attention spans will be short, and they will be easily distracted. Try to hook viewers within fifteen seconds and let them go after no more than five minutes.

Design Principle 4: Match the Media

Some people are Facebook people. Some are Twitter people. Some go to portal sites. The fact is, each person has his or her own media preferences. Therefore, it helps to mix up the media that you use and coordinate your efforts to drive people to the social media that enable them to act.

First, to engage the broadest audience possible, you must leverage both online and offline media. The Obama campaign team proved to be masters at this. The team garnered 5 million supporters on fifteen different social networks ranging from Facebook to Disaboom. The team also leveraged such technologies as email (one billion emails sent!) and texts (to 3 million mobile and SMS subscribers). They created, tested, and emailed 8,000 to 10,000 unique messages targeted to specific segments of their 13-million-member email list. On Election Day, the campaign used Twitter to post toll-free numbers and information to help find polling locations as well as volunteer opportunities. Moreover, in battleground states, if people went to the website to look up their polling places, the site would list five other people who had the same polling place and encouraged the supporter to call them or knock on their doors and take them along.

The team also created offline opportunities so that people could physically, rather than just virtually, become involved. One example was Walk for Change, a large national grassroots canvassing program that proved very successful. The beauty of the effort was in how everything intertwined: the canvass events were planned by Obama supporters who had signed up on the campaign's email list or had signed in on MyBO and organized an event. This symbiotic relationship of online and offline events was truly new. In the past, these efforts would have been handled by different teams and been managed in completely different ways. By harnessing the immediacy of online to the visceral impact of offline, Obama took campaigning to a new level.

One benefit of mixing media, matching distinct media types with distinct audiences, is that it allows you to build opportunities for conversations, feedback, and the collective

TOMS Shoes

In 2006 Blake Mycoskie, a Los Angeles entrepreneur and traveler, perhaps best known for finishing third on the Amazing Race II, found during a trip through Argentina that the children typically did not have shoes to protect their feet. Wanting to help, he created TOMS Shoes (http://www.tomshoes.com), a for-profit California company that would use the purchasing power of individuals to benefit the greater good. Mycoskie vowed to give a pair of new shoes to a child in need for every pair he sold. One for One, he called it.

In the first year, he sold ten thousand pairs of his shoes and returned to Argentina with a group of family, friends, and staff to distribute ten thousand more. His product, which has expanded beyond shoes, has become available online and in more than five hundred stores internationally, including Nordstrom's and Whole Foods, and is endorsed by celebrities including Karl Lagerfeld and Scarlett Johansson.

To fully engage its customers, TOMS relies on two discrete types of media. The first is social media. With its own YouTube channel, TOMS highlights its cause with real stories of the children whose lives were changed by receiving the shoes, and encourages contributions of user-generated content related to TOMS products. The TOMS Facebook page features user-generated videos of the brand's good deeds, and tracks and honors the fans who forward the videos to others; its Twitter page has a following of 300,000.

However, TOMS also sponsors offline events. The TOMS Vagabond tour, which was sponsored in 2008 by the Dave Matthews Band, moves from college town to college town to spread the word about the organization's good work. And TOMS organizes an annual barefoot-for-a-day event; shoe "drops," where customers and volunteers go on the trips to hand-deliver the shoes; design-your-own-shoe contests; and other interactive events that engage the target audience.

No doubt TOMS has engaged an audience—and made a difference. Since its founding in May 2006, TOMS has given more than 600,000 pairs of shoes to children in Argentina, Ethiopia, Haiti, South Africa, and the United States. The company hopes to give away more than one million pairs of shoes by 2012.

creation of brands and ideas. Engagement and empowerment are best achieved when information flows in both directions. Rather than just writing a case study and disseminating it, or creating an audio or video story or plea for help and broadcasting it to the world, you need to enable rapid feedback and iteration.

Collective creation, and thus engagement, take practice. Those of us accustomed to traditional media tend to think of our efforts as works of individual art, not as a community mural. We tend to be defensive in the face of feedback, and that just doesn't work in new media.

There are two important enablers to this new way of thinking: platforms and mind-set. The platform aspect is mechanical, and the plethora of social Web tools makes it easy to place your ideas in locations where feedback is not just possible but encouraged. For example, think blogs, websites, or even places such as the popular T-shirt site threadless.com or quirky.com, where the community actually creates the product from start to finish, and the "winning" final product is voted on and produced in limited editions to the crowd's specifications.

The mind-set aspect is more fundamental. In some cases, feedback and fine-tuning are what's required. Return to the question you're trying to answer or the problem you're seeking to solve before posting an answer to viewers' reactions to your marketing messages. Put the question or the problem to your audience; ask for their ideas. You will probably be surprised by what comes back. The easier you make it for them to contribute, the better. But don't stop there. True engagement follows this step after you acknowledge, integrate, and sincerely thank people for their submissions and feedback. For extra credit, ask them to help you make decisions by voting on final contenders.

> ## Four Design Principles to Engage
>
> ### TEAM
>
> **Tell a story.** Find compelling, sticky stories to convey critical information. Remember: less is more.
>
> **Empathize.** As you engage, let your audience engage you. What is important to them? How does that relate to your campaign?
>
> **Be Authentic.** True passion is contagious. The more authentic you come across, the easier it will be for others to connect with you and your cause. Emphasize your shared values and beliefs.
>
> **Match the media.** *How* and *where* we say something can be as important as what we say. Align communication and context.

Charity: Water Engages

Scott Harrison—a nightclub and fashion promoter who excelled at bringing models and hedge-fund kings together and then selling them $500 bottles of vodka in cavernous spaces—was at the top of his world. He had money, power, and beautiful girlfriends. There was something else that came with the lifestyle too, though: he felt "spiritually bankrupt" and miserable. Desperately unhappy, he wanted to change.

He constantly wondered, What would the opposite of my life look like? In a search for that answer, he signed up to volunteer aboard a floating hospital that offered free medical care in the world's poorest nations. He traded his spacious midtown loft for a 150-square-foot cabin with bunk beds, roommates, and cockroaches. The upscale restaurants he frequented were replaced by a mess hall that served four hundred people.

Harrison traveled to Africa, serving as the ship's photojournalist, and soon began to see a very different world from the one he knew. Upon arrival at a port, the ship's medical staff would show pictures of the deformities and diseases that they could alleviate, and thousands of people would flock looking for an answer to a debilitating problem—an enormous tumor, a cleft lip and palate, flesh eaten by bacteria from water-borne diseases. Harrison's camera lens brought astonishing poverty and pain into focus, and he began documenting people's struggles, and their courage.

After eight months, Harrison moved back to New York, but did not return to his former life. Aware that many of the diseases and medical problems he saw while traveling stemmed from inadequate access to clean drinking water, he founded Charity: Water, a nonprofit that would bring clean and safe drinking water to people in developing nations.

Harrison launched the organization on his thirty-first birthday and asked friends to donate $31 instead of giving him a gift, as a way to make a difference. It worked: the birthday generated $15,000 and helped build Charity: Water's first few wells in Uganda. In the three years that followed, Harrison's simple birthday wish resulted in $13 million raised; 1,548 water projects; and more than eight hundred thousand people who have benefited from clean water.

The reasons for Charity: Water's success can be explained through the four design principles of Engage. The first method Harrison employed was telling a story. His personal story—one that evokes themes of redemption, change, and hope—engages others on an emotional level. Harrison, who comes off as a thoughtful and accessible thirty-something, candidly discusses in media interviews and on YouTube videos why and how he started the organization. Viewers fall in love with him and his cause as he shows his audience what's possible.

Charity: Water has found a way to evoke empathy, the second principle to Engage, through the use of photographs and videos that reveal the urgency of the water situation in the developing world. The use of visual images has been a pivotal part of the campaign process since the group's founding, when

---

It's a Small Wired World

Jade Clavier, an eight-year-old girl, saw the inspirational Charity: Water video that founder Scott Harrison developed for his thirty-first birthday. She was shaken by the realization that kids in Africa have to drink muddy water instead of the clean water that she had always taken for granted. She also felt empowered: there was one simple thing she could do.

Jade decided to ask for $9 or more from everyone she knew. This effort resulted in meeting her goal of raising $200. She extended her campaign using mycharitywater.com, the organization's custom-built social networking and fundraising tool, to spread the word about her cause, collect donations, share updates, and track progress. And she doubled her efforts: "Now my Christmas wish is to help even more people. With $20 you can help one kid get clean water for the next 20 years. How many kids can we help together? Please join me in helping them," she wrote on her Charity: Water page.

Her father highlighted her goal in his blog; her mother shared the campaign through her Facebook and Twitter accounts. "If you—like us—find that this is an important cause to support, please help spreading the word or consider donating to Jade's wish." Jade raised nearly $2,000.

Next stop (and a surprise for Jade): her parents hope to take the whole family to the village where a well is being built.

An homage to the power of social technology.

it funded six wells in Uganda—and took pictures of them. Instead of relying on statistics and numbers, the organization promotes compelling stories from that community to their audience back home: stories of a fifteen-year-old boy in Murinja, Rwanda, who no longer walks five times a day with a twenty-pound Jerry Can on his head to get necessary water; a mother in Uganda who now has water to grow vegetables, clean her children's uniforms, and bathe; the people of Rio Platano, Honduras, who are no longer getting sick from contaminated water. Charity: Water uses events to get other people to empathize, including its use of outdoor exhibitions where dirty water is displayed. People are forced to think about what it would be like to live without access to clean water.

The campaign evokes the third principle of Engage, be authentic, through its commitment to transparency. Donors give knowing where their money is going—and, through the reports and updates on the website, they are connected to the results.

Finally, Charity: Water excels at matching the media to its message. The group has a staff member dedicated to updating the various social media platforms regularly, and creating distinctive messages for Twitter and Facebook fan pages. They also rely heavily on video. One of the most effective video projects involved convincing Terry George, the director of *Hotel Rwanda,* to make a sixty-second public service announcement for Charity: Water, in which movie star Jennifer Connelly takes a forty-pound gasoline can to Central Park, fills it with dirty water from the lagoon, and brings it home to serve to her two children. Charity: Water even managed to convince the producers of *American Idol* to broadcast the spot during the show, ensuring that more than 25 million viewers saw it.

Getting Started with Engage

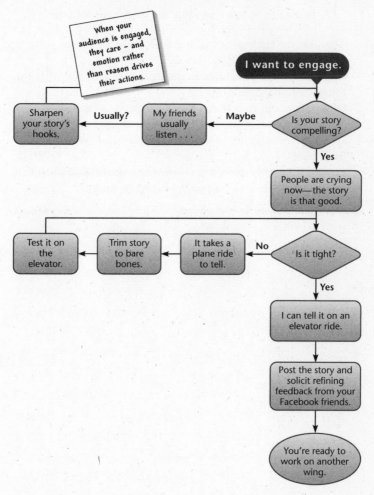

By calling on the four principles of Engage, Charity: Water demonstrates how you can make others fall in love with your cause. This is the penultimate wing of the Dragonfly Effect. It will help you prime your audience for the next step: inspiring them to take action.

Exercises to Strengthen the "Engagement Muscle"

1. When was the last time you offered to do someone a favor (even though he didn't ask)? Why did you?
2. What was the last great book you read or movie you saw? What got your attention and then kept it?
3. Tell a favorite story to a friend. Watch her closely. What seems to engage her? At what points does she seem less engaged?
4. Recall when you last fell in love. What did it feel like? Why did you fall in love?
5. Ask yourself what your most powerful motivator is. What kind of appeal is most likely to get your attention and keep it?

WING 4
Take Action

How to Empower Others, Enable Them—and Cultivate a Movement

As we look ahead to the next century, leaders will be those who empower others.

—BILL GATES

In many ways, Alex Scott was a regular kid. Her favorite food was French fries; her favorite color, blue. She hoped to be a fashion designer one day. But in other ways—perhaps most ways—Alex was different. Just before her first birthday, Alex was diagnosed with neuroblastoma, an aggressive form of childhood cancer. A tumor was removed from her back, and doctors told her parents, Liz and Jay, that if she beat the cancer she would likely not walk again. Two weeks later Alex moved her leg—one of the many early clues about her determination and capabilities.

When Alex was four, after receiving a stem cell transplant, she came up with a plan that would change how she and her family coped with cancer from then on. "When I get out of the hospital I want to have a lemonade stand," she said. Alex wanted to use the money she made to fight cancer and help other children.

Her parents admit now that they laughed. (Not a bad reaction . . . we know that laughter in the midst of challenge is good.) Admittedly, it was an unlikely proposition. Although one in every 330 American children contracts cancer before age twenty, childhood cancer research is consistently underfunded.[1] Alex was advised that it could be challenging to raise money fifty cents at a time. "I don't care; I'll do it anyway," she replied.

Alex set up a table in her front yard, and like thousands of other junior entrepreneurs around the country, started selling paper cups of lemonade to neighbors and passersby. Her hand-printed sign advertised (along with the price of the lemonade) that all proceeds would go to childhood cancer research. The fifty-cent price was ignored as customers paid with bills ($1, $5, $10, and $20) and allowed her to keep the change as a donation. (Alex understood the importance of change management, and the change really added up—similar to Bank of America's Keep the Change program, which allows customers to round up their debit card purchases to the nearest dollar, and deposit the difference into their savings accounts. Of course, Alex did it first.)

True to her word, Alex raised more than $2,000 from her first lemonade stand. She reopened her stand for business each summer, and news of its existence and worthy cause spread far beyond her neighborhood, her town, and even her home state of Pennsylvania. She leveraged that momentum and got others to set up their own lemonade stands. Her approach was sticky

in more ways than one. Before long, lemonade stand fund-
raisers took place in each of the fifty states, plus Canada and
France. Alex and her family appeared on the *Oprah Winfrey
Show* as well as the *Today Show.*

Not one to be easily daunted, Alex set a goal to raise $1
million for cancer research. By the time she reached $700,000,
Volvo of North America stepped in and pledged to hold a
fundraising event to assure that the $1 million goal would be
reached.

Four years after setting up her first lemonade stand, Alex
succumbed to cancer. She was eight. In her too-short life she
raised $1 million for cancer research, built awareness of the
seriousness of childhood cancer, and taught a generation of
children (and their parents) about the importance of abstract
ideals like community and charity. She also demonstrated that
making a difference can be fun.

To carry on Alex's legacy, her parents established a nonprofit in her name, Alex's Lemonade Stand Foundation (ALSF).
Since its founding, the 501(c)3 charity has inspired more than
ten thousand volunteers to set up more than fifteen thousand
stands. As of January 2010 it's raised an excess of $27 million
and donated to more than one hundred research projects at
nearly fifty institutions in the United States. Alex assembled a
band of cancer-fighting evangelists (family, friends, neighbors,
citizens, corporations) that was far more powerful than anyone,
even those closest to her, ever thought possible. ALSF called
people to action, and grew exponentially, with the help of social media, which allowed the organization to garner a strong
and faithful fan base—30,000 Twitter followers and 33,000
Facebook fans. People all over the world took Alex's idea and
transformed it into a movement.[2]

From Newsletters to Social Media: The Story of Alex's Lemonade Stand Foundation

Initially, ALSF stayed connected to its constituents through two electronic newsletters, "Million Dollar Monday" and "Freshly Squeezed Friday News," which included updates and anecdotes from lemonade stands around the country. No explicit appeal was made; the group kept the news light and fun. But when ALSF started branching into social media, it found that the old rules didn't apply.

Timing is everything. Most scheduled tweets go out every hour on the hour. ALSF found that if they sent a tweet at fifteen minutes past the hour, given Twitter's scrolling layout, it was more likely to stay on-screen longer. To avoid viewer fatigue, the ALSF community manager tweets for twelve hours, then takes twelve hours off before starting again.

Facebook and Twitter are different species. ASLF learned that whereas Facebook users love to comment and interact in an indirect manner, happy to see others discussing the things they are interested in, Twitter followers want more direct interaction with the person behind the tweets and get excited when they're mentioned. In addition, the organizers found that on Facebook it was better to have a unified brand-centered voice, whereas on Twitter they achieved better engagement with a more personal, casual tone.

Less is more. Built-in analytics made it easy for ALSF to learn what works on YouTube. For example, the footage of its 5K LemonRun was originally six minutes, but the hot-spot analytics helped the organizers realize exactly when viewers lost interest. Editing it down to one-and-a-half minutes kept viewers engaged. Based on feedback, ALSF cut down non-Twitter contact frequency to once or twice daily. It also recognized the need to be sensitive of the time zones of those receiving Facebook and email updates, so as not to bombard subscribers. Although many supporters are happy to hear from the foundation more than once a day, they do not want to wake up to an inbox full of ALSF items to clear!

Inspiring Action

The success of Alex's Lemonade Stand Foundation wasn't as much about raising money as it was inspiring people to take action. By helping children around the country set up their own lemonade stands to fight childhood cancer, Alex mobilized a population of young ambassadors whose involvement and heightened awareness made a much more significant impact.

The organization embraced all four wings of the dragonfly: it *focused* on the goal of honoring Alex's wish to raise money to fight childhood cancer; it *grabbed attention* by tapping into a deep-rooted American tradition, the lemonade stand, owning a color (yellow), and creating sticky subbrands (including LemonRun and "Freshly Squeezed Friday News"); it *engaged* people's emotions by telling Alex's compelling story. And finally, it excelled at the fourth wing of the Dragonfly Effect, Take Action, the wing critical to closing the loop on previous efforts by enabling others to easily start their own lemonade stands and become part of the solution.

When you grab people's attention, they sit up and listen. When you engage people, you connect with them and inspire them. However, too many efforts just stop there, leaving people with good intentions that may never be acted on. What was critical in the case of Alex's Lemonade Stand Foundation was how it enabled action by providing its audience with the tools to get them to *do* something. Take Action is about requiring individuals to exert themselves and to make the transition beyond being interested by what you have to say to actually doing something about it. After all, in a world where a blanket with sleeves constitutes a hot-ticket item, it's hard to get people off the couch.

The final wing is pivotal, but far from simple. You need to know what to ask for and how to ask for it. Second, you must listen to how the audience responds so that you can continually integrate their reactions and feedback, honing and refining your message and sometimes the offering itself. But before we dive into these two skills, we'll define a *call to action*.

A Call to Action

"Call in the next five minutes to get this special price." "Quantities are limited, so act now!" You're likely no stranger to the call to action—the message at the end of a commercial when someone oozing with urgency tells you what to do.

The call to action at the end of sales and marketing materials has traditionally been embraced by marketers as a way to convert mere prospects into customers. They provide audiences with participative next steps that move them closer and closer to making a purchase. Many calls to action fail (and not just the cheesy, clichéd ones) because they don't offer anything more compelling than a "P.S." urging the recipient to call a certain phone number or click on a URL. That's not a call to action; that's a feeble whimper.

Unfortunately, nonprofit organizations are making these mistakes too. Worse, many are even less sophisticated—failing to provide even the minimal calls to action that their for-profit counterparts do. Nonprofits routinely try to disseminate information about their causes without providing specific instructions on how the interested parties should *act*. (Many of us incorrectly believe that simply providing information will be more effective than asking outright.[3]) Technology companies tend to fall into this trap too, expecting that clear, objective disclosure of features and functions will speak for themselves, that the choice will be self-evident. It usually isn't. Further, organizations often fail to use social networking to create a sense of community with their educational campaigns. That's a missed opportunity. People like to consult with others before devoting money or time to a cause; they want to ensure that their money and time will be well spent. (This phenomenon explains the popularity of the ratings systems of Amazon.com, where users "grade" books and other retail products, or Yelp, which does the same for local businesses and services.)

When organizations do combine the power of the call to action with innovative social media tools, they can achieve extraordinary results. Take the campaign Take a Bite Out of IHOP's Animal Cruelty, which the Humane Society of the United States launched to try to get the restaurant chain to use cage-free eggs. The Humane Society used Facebook's status-tagging features to ask their 170,000-plus Facebook fans to tag IHOP when they changed their status or posted a new message to express their outrage about what it perceived as IHOP's inhumane practices.[4] This had an immediate and powerful effect. As the campaign went viral, more and more people tagged status updates. The posts showed up on IHOP's fan page, where it had 57,000 fans (which translates into a lot of eggs). Within six weeks, IHOP was forced to address the issue,[5] and its executives have since agreed to test the use of cage-free eggs and promised to switch millions of eggs to cage-free if the testing proved successful.

The Psychology of Asking

You get that you have to make an ask—that you must literally *compel* the audience into action. But how? There are many different types of asks, but only one constant: what you are asking of people must be highly focused, absolutely specific, and oriented to action, so as to avoid overwhelming your audience. Behavior change occurs when the behavior is easy to do.[6] Research suggests that when it comes to encouraging others to help, small asks often lead to better results. Offering diverse opportunities to contribute to your cause over time and regularly communicating new ways to get involved can lead to donor satisfaction and raise more money.[7] As we discussed in Wing 1, specific manageable goals help people enjoy a task more.[8] You can empower others by keeping your request focused.

We have observed three effects at work when it comes to using social media to drive others to take action for a cause. First, setting up a social Web presence to solicit donations is so easy that it has led to a proliferation of money asks. Second, social media users expect transparency, so we are seeing much more data on fundraising progress than we have ever been privy to before. Third, as we see in the best examples, social media are far more than fundraising tools. Social networks are particularly effective at increasing motivation,[9] and they enable us to quickly create a critical mass of supporters who then serve as agents for action. Although effective use of social media in the nonprofit sector varies dramatically across organizations, thinking of the benefits beyond fundraising is a smart way to expand reach and impact, as the nonprofit social media expert Beth Kanter points out.[10] We couldn't agree more.

The Nike WE Portal:
A Fresh Look at What You Can Ask For

Already known for its corporate philanthropic and social responsibility efforts, Nike wanted to empower its thirty thousand employees around the world to share their personal philanthropic causes. Nike launched its WE Portal in July 2009 with the hope that by leveraging mass collaboration enabled by Web 2.0 technologies the company could answer the question, "how can we enable employees to give back easily, in their own way, and then get out of their way?"

The Nike team developed a human-centered design, with a focus on the individual driving the direction, and the corporation taking a backseat. They structured the Nike WE Portal so that employees' donations could fall into four categories: time, voice, money, and talent. Points accrue on each employee's WE profile page as a badge of honor, and can be exchanged for gifts of money or products to the approved charity of the employee's choice. Approximately 60 percent of the projects in the Nike WE Portal were chosen by Nike on the basis of its corporate philanthropic goals and priorities; the other 40 percent were suggested by the employees themselves. Nike has created a portal that supports the ways in which its employees want to give, and affords them a sense of ownership.

The Nike WE Portal matches each employee with opportunities to give back by asking him his location and his passion. In addition to communicating through the WE blog and capturing and posting employee feedback, Nike has begun to add social networking features, such as people search and the ability to follow other employees, to help employees get more ideas and inspiration for ways to give back.

In just six months since its inception, the Nike WE Portal program has recruited more than three thousand employees to participate, get involved, and give back—and in a way that involves Nike.[11]

What to Ask For?

Nonprofits suffer as much as businesses from economic down-turns. Donations at two-thirds of public charities declined in 2008, according to the Giving USA Foundation.[12] This represents the first decrease in donations in current dollars since 1987, and only the second year-over-year giving slump since the organization began publishing its annual reports fifty-two years ago. In a similar vein, the amount of time volunteers have donated to causes has been flat for several years, according to the Corporation for National and Community Service.[13] Given these trends, nonprofits are constantly searching for ways to increase both the number of donors and the amount of time or money that donors offer. They have three strategic issues to consider: what to ask for, how to ask for it, and when to ask for it. Correctly combining these factors can determine whether you meet, exceed, or fall short of your goal. The rest of this chapter will focus on how to design your ask to achieve the most effective results.

Picking the Right Type of Ask

Research assessing why people volunteer time and contribute money to charitable causes found that the number one reason is that "they were asked by someone,"[14] which suggests that the way you ask matters. But it's not enough to simply ask for time, money, or both. You need to carefully calculate the what, how, when, and scope of your ask to yield maximum results. Whether you ask for or require participation should be based on two factors: your degree of separation from the potential donor and the emotional intensity of your ask. If you're socially close to a potential donor and the emotional intensity is high (your friend is battling an aggressive form of cancer), you are in a position to simply *tell* him or her to participate. These are your family members and close friends; they trust you and want to help you. If the emotional intensity is relatively low ("let's work together to stop climate change"), you should approach them with an *ask,* not a tell. (The reason: without the emotional component, it should be up to potential donors' discretion whether they care to be involved. Still, you ought to be able to count on a close friend or relative for at least a small contribution.)

When the social distance is great (between you and Brad Pitt, for example), and the emotional intensity high, you can *require* participation and hope that your potential supporter is as moved to act as you are. This works best in movements inspired by outrage—for example, those fighting against inhumane treatment of children or animals. If the cause is less emotionally intense, then a softer ask, such as an invitation, will be more effective.

How to Ask

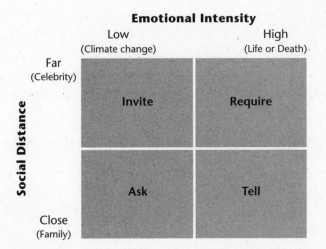

	Emotional Intensity	
	Low (Climate change)	High (Life or Death)
Far (Celebrity)	Invite	Require
Close (Family)	Ask	Tell

Social Distance

Try using the framework above as a litmus test. For example, imagine you're running for Team in Training (the Leukemia & Lymphoma Society's charity sports training program) and are soliciting support from friends. The social distance is very close, but the emotional intensity is low, so it would be a straightforward ask. In contrast, if you are soliciting support from executives at your corporation (social distance is far), think in terms of an invitation. However, if your child has leukemia, you have a license to require. In that case, if you are soliciting your friends, it would be a tell. Remember, they are your support network, and you would do the same for them.

No person is too high on the social, economic, or political scale to approach for your cause. No matter how socially distant an individual is, it is worth asking him or her. Endorsements by public figures have been proven to raise the profile of charities and spread awareness.[15] Princess Diana, who supported almost a hundred charities, humanitarian organizations, and civic groups during her lifetime, most visibly with her efforts to ban land mines, helped raise an estimated $450 million each year.[16] Public figures' endorsement of nonprofit causes has been rising over the years. Don't be afraid to tell them you *need* them. So many people tiptoe nervously around celebrities, treating them as if they were not quite human, that anyone who treats them as peers is likely to stand out. Give it a shot—you have nothing to lose.

Differentiate Between First and Second Asks

One thing to strategize constantly is how a first action will lead to a second action, and so on. If you've settled on a strategy of "micro participation," as Kiva has, how do you construct your ask so that a single action becomes the first rung of a ladder into a long-term relationship? You must specify what you want people to do right now, even as you anticipate and provide further opportunities for them to become even more involved.

Free trials of products or services can serve as a first rung. In a five-minute video on the social networking site Ignite (sponsored by O'Reilly Media), Alexis Bauer beautifully illustrated the

ProFounder: Crowdfunding for Small Business

Jessica Jackley (of Kiva) and Dana Mauriello had heard countless stories of entrepreneurs who could not get bank loans to pursue their dreams and were considering very high interest credit as a last resort. Their big insight was that most entrepreneurs are surrounded by supportive communities that, with the right tools (social media being optimal), could be leveraged to help. There is $129 billion in "friends and family" funding each year—that's 87 percent of all private financing, beating out formal sources like venture capital by orders of magnitude. But this money usually comes from a handful of people putting in large amounts. Jackley and Mauriello decided to try to change the paradigm. What would happen, they thought, if lots of people contributed small amounts instead?

Enter ProFounder, a "crowdfunding" platform created to address the problem of small business financing in the United States. Entrepreneurs design an offer that includes a 0 percent interest loan paid back monthly, plus an annual reward that is a percentage of their revenue. The entrepreneur's story, pitch, and term sheet go on a private fundraising website for the company, which the entrepreneur can then share with her community via Facebook, Twitter, YouTube-placed videos, and other social media. By leveraging human-centered design, sticky tools for connectivity, and storytelling, ProFounder has morphed into more than just a path to cash. Investors get an annual reward—either as a dividend payment or a redirected grant to a nonprofit (and eventually to the ProFounder's Entrepreneur's Fund). It's a virtuous cycle, empowering entrepreneurs and enabled by social technology.

ladder concept. Check out "How to Work a Crowd," in which Bauer explains how to plant conversational seeds in a room full of strangers. The first time you talk to a person you are a stranger, she explains. But after you've moved around the room and planted numerous other seeds, when you come back to that person, you are no longer a stranger but a familiar face—and the next time, you're greeted as friend, one trusted enough to introduce that person to other "friends" you've made during your rounds.[17]

Ask for Time (Before Money)

We've already seen how political campaigns and nonprofits have effectively used the social Web to achieve what would have been impossible only a few years ago. When Areej Khan wanted to ignite a debate on the ban on women drivers in Saudi Arabia, she didn't seek monetary contributions; she simply asked individuals to write their opinions on stickers that could be uploaded and circulated on Flickr and offline as bumper stickers. Ultimately, her To Drive or Not to Drive effort started an important dialogue both online and offline. Help Sameer and Help Vinay encouraged thousands of people to join the bone marrow registry and never asked for any money. "Vinay felt that by accepting money, you were telling people that it was okay not to go and register," says Priti Radhakrishnan, who ran Help Vinay. "We were really focused on our goal, and money wouldn't have gotten us there."

Research has found that when you ask for time, your product or cause can become more alluring and better liked.[18] The *time-ask effect* shows that focusing your message on time (versus money) can affect your audience's willingness to contribute. We conducted experiments, both in the lab and in the field, which revealed that asking individuals to think about

The American Lung Cancer Foundation and the Time-Ask Effect: Why You Should Ask People to Donate Time!

In 2008, Wendy Liu (UCLA) and Jennifer Aaker (Stanford) conducted a study in which ordinary consumers from all over the United States were asked to help fight lung cancer. Participants were given materials that read, "Lung cancer is the leading cancer killer in both men and women in the United States. The American Lung Cancer Foundation's mission is to promote public awareness, policy making, and medical research towards preventing lung cancer."

They were told that the foundation was having a fundraising event. Half the participants were asked, "How much time would you like to donate to the American Lung Cancer Foundation?" (The other participants were not asked the volunteering question.) Next, both groups were asked, "How much money would you donate to the American Lung Cancer Foundation?" The results proved the power of the time-ask effect. When participants were not questioned about their willingness to donate time before being asked about the monetary pledge, the average level of donation was $24.46. However, when they were, this amount increased nearly 50 percent, to $36.44. These results replicate with real money. People give about one-and-a-half to two times as much when you ask them to volunteer time before asking for money.

There are a few explanations for the time-ask effect. One is the guilt many people feel after declining to volunteer, which may be assuaged by donating more money.[20] However, the results did not support a guilt-based explanation; those who said they would give less time also gave less money. Instead, a request for time seemed to trigger an emotional mind-set. People imagined themselves volunteering and, even though they actually hadn't, felt an emotional investment. The resulting halo effect then drove them to give more money. People motivated by happiness or empathy are more likely to become repeat donors than those motivated by guilt.

how much time they would like to donate to a charity actually increases the amount of money they ultimately contribute to the cause.[19] (See the preceding box for more details.)

There's important related research on happiness. Studies have found that younger people see happiness as an excited, high-arousal feeling, whereas older people perceive happiness as a peaceful, content feeling. This transition as people age may be caused by feelings of connectedness with other people.[21] The meaning of happiness varies across cultures (and religions) as well. People from individualistic cultures, such as European Americans (and Christians), are more likely to value excitement, whereas people from collectivist cultures, such as East Asians (and Buddhists), value calm.[22] Part of the success of Alex's Lemonade Stand Foundation can be attributed to its ability to draw in diverse cultures and age groups through its community-building activities. ALSF creates ongoing excitement and fosters a sense of connection that contributes to the project's sustainability. By focusing on asking for time versus money, the group successfully gains traction with different audiences and spurs them into action.

Asking for time activates an emotional mind-set that makes well-being and happiness more easily accessible—thus leading to donations.[23] When people are solicited for their time, they are more likely to think in terms of emotional meaning and fulfillment: "Will volunteering for this charity make me happy?" When tapped for money, they start thinking about the far more practical, boring, and sometimes painful matter of economic utility: "Will donating money make a dent in my wallet?" Thinking about money makes people become less helpful to others and makes them want to play and work alone.[24]

The Dragonfly Encyclopedia of Asks, following, explores the many different types of asks and how to employ them effectively.

The Dragonfly Encyclopedia of Asks

The indirect (implied) ask can be more persuasive than direct asks.[25] Thus, stating that "children are starving in Africa" might well be more effective than asking, "Will you give money to buy food for African children?" Simply asking for help without giving elaborate explanations or reasons is successful on occasion, however. Never underestimate the extent to which people will comply with a simple request due to the social awkwardness, difficulty, and embarrassment of saying no.[26]

The reciprocity ask involves offering something in return for a donation. For example, when the Disabled American Veterans organization mails out requests with sets of free personalized address labels, their success rate doubles from 18 to 35 percent.[27] Offering a fun activity is probably the best variation of this ask—for example, Avon's walks to raise money for breast cancer or the annual AIDS/Lifecycle bike ride between San Francisco and Los Angeles.

The concession ask is a related strategy, in which you request a major commitment first and then, after being rejected, ask for something less onerous. Take this example: When random passersby were asked to help chaperone juvenile detention center inmates on a day trip to the zoo, 17 percent said yes. Yet when researchers first asked if they would volunteer two hours per week as an unpaid counselor for the center—an ask that everyone rejected—and then asked if they would chaperone a zoo visit, they got a 50 percent acceptance rate.[28]

The social validation ask is when you show potential donors that their peers are contributing to your cause. Donors to a public radio station who were told what others had contributed gave two or three times more than those who were not informed.

The competitive ask leverages competitive urges by emphasizing how one donor or participant in a cause stacks up against others in the community. Kiva provides an example of this, as does Foursquare.com, which offers its "super users" special privileges.

The authoritative ask falls on the firmer, more serious end of the ask spectrum and relies on quoting scientific studies, getting an expert to endorse your cause, or enlisting a celebrity spokesperson.

Design Principles to Empower Others to Take Action

Design Principle 1: Make It Easy

The reality of today's world is that many people simply don't have a lot of time to give to a cause. You have to be sensitive to this, or you will have trouble attracting and retaining active participants. By demonstrating that you value their time and by making efficient use of their contributions—perhaps by precisely matching tasks to their particular interest or skill set—you can simultaneously boost their effectiveness while giving them a greater sense of accomplishment. This increases the likelihood that they will continue to participate.

Helping people achieve small goals leads them naturally to adopt more ambitious behaviors, often without a bigger intervention. For example, if the big goal is to convince people to be more environmentally friendly, ask them to do something small first. Suggest that they change a single light bulb in their home. Let them breathe for a moment, basking in their success, and then intervene again, expanding the effort by making the target behavior more difficult. Perhaps you might suggest that they replace *all* the inefficient light bulbs in their home.[29]

The Extraordinaries, which Ben Rigby was inspired to cofound after reading that nearly half of respondents to a poll cited lack of time as the main reason they didn't volunteer, demonstrates the value of the small, easy ask. The organization has captured a unique opportunity by providing people with a way to put downtime to good use. Rather than interrupt their supporters when they're trying to do something else and asking them to take an action then (what Seth Godin refers to as "interruption marketing"), the Extraordinaries allows people to choose a cause and an activity (for example, identifying elements in images for the Smithsonian) and volunteer at their convenience. People download the Extraordinaries iPhone application and forget about it until they have five or ten minutes on their hands to micro-volunteer.

This effort is all about empowering potential volunteers or donors and keeping them from feeling overtaxed or overwhelmed. Yahoo! excelled at this with its You In? campaign, launched over the 2009 holidays. You In? attempted to enlist its employees—famous for being young and hip—to engage

Be Concrete

Consider the following social experiment. Dustin Curtis wanted to encourage readers of his popular blog to also follow him on Twitter. At first, he simply made a quiet announcement on the blog that he was now on Twitter and included a link. By rewording his announcement as an imperative, "Follow me on Twitter!" he increased click-throughs by more than 50 percent. He gradually increased the strength of his messaging, incrementally boosting the click-throughs with ever-stronger language. Finally, telling readers to "Click here" increased click-throughs by another 25 percent. By being more direct and forceful, Curtis was able to improve overall click-throughs to his Twitter account by 173 percent.

in random acts of kindness and in doing so to create ripple effects. The campaign was easy to understand and even easier for individuals to envision themselves joining. Employees who performed acts of kindness were encouraged to post their stories on the Yahoo! For Good website, or their videos or pictures to a linked Yahoo! Flickr group. Typical acts of kindness included topping off a parking meter, paying a toll for the car behind, and shoveling snow. Yahoo! employees from eighteen countries participated, submitting over 300,000 status updates of random acts of kindness.

Finally, consider how Alex's Lemonade Stand Foundation has embraced many tactics—and established an entire process—that makes it very simple for someone to participate. Once an individual goes to the ALSF website to sign up to run a "lemanade" (Alex's spelling) stand, he or she completes a simple form and is immediately sent a "lemanade stand in a box" set, which includes cups, banners, and balloons. Within fifteen minutes of signing up, parents (ourselves included) receive an email from ALSF public relations staff offering help to establish media contacts to promote the stand in local media. Parents are sent a press release template, which they are encouraged to personalize, not just with logistical information (time and location of their lemonade stand event), but with personal reasons for running the lemonade stand, to add authenticity, depth, and color to the story. For example, our kids included their pet issues: ending swine flu, alleviating croup, and supporting the Make-a-Wish Foundation, which made their story more personal and therefore compelling.

You want participation. The only way to get it—especially at first—is to make it easy. Always ask for participation in "bite-size" chunks or provide easy-to-follow instructions on how to contribute to a cause.

How to Make Behavior Change Easy

Make the ask small and concrete. People won't know what to do if your request is too abstract. An open-ended ask to "save the planet" will never be as effective as a campaign that asks people to use energy-saving lightbulbs and even provides some to them for free.

Offer a kit that contains templates. Don't expect contributors to reinvent what previous contributors have done. Make sure any grunt work has been done, and incorporate advice and best practices so that new contributors benefit from others' experience.

Encourage reuse of material. Imitation is the highest and most sincere compliment, and in motivating people to take action for your cause, this is no exception. Encourage constant communication to stay aware of what's working best in the field. Spread success stories, and encourage people to adapt tools and techniques to achieve similar successes.

Design Principle 2: Make It Fun

We know we're talking about some very serious topics in this book, but we can't ignore an important and possibly surprising element of social movements: the fueling effect of fun. Fun has an important place in curing cancer, solving the climate crisis, and alleviating poverty. It will make your endeavor not only more tolerable for you but also a whole lot stickier for your audience. (And, ultimately, that's what this is all about—getting your audience to do something.)

Consider the success of a viral marketing campaign from Volkswagen Sweden and DDB Stockholm, themed Rolighetsteorin, or Fun Theory, which infuses fun into everyday activities to encourage people to do the right thing (and ultimately positions Volkswagen and its new environmentally friendly BlueMotion Technologies brand by helping consumers make the leap that its cars are good for the environment as well as fun for the driver). Volkswagen thinks consumers can have it all, so to speak, and it believes that "fun is the easiest way to change people's behavior for the better."[30]

In one of the videos, Volkswagen has a crew come in late at night and turn the stairs next to an escalator at a train station into a giant piano. Suddenly, the stairs seem fun to use—so much so that the number of commuters who chose the stairs over the escalator increased by 66 percent.

In another video, the crew wires a regular trash can with motion-activated depth sound effects, so that when someone tosses in some trash, it sounds as though it's falling a long way until there's the sound of a final splat. People are so surprised and delighted they even start picking up other people's garbage to experience the fun again. Next on the campaign: a glass bottle recycling game machine. "By making driving and the world more fun, we turn the VW brand into a hero," DDB Stockholm deputy manager Lars Axelsson said in the *Los Angeles Times*. "Our experiments and our *Fun Theory* films make the world a better and more fun place to live."

Volkswagen continues to extend the fun (and its message) through social media. The video clip of people skipping the escalator in favor of composing music on the piano stairs of the Odenplan subway station in Stockholm, Sweden, got more than 500,000 views on YouTube within two weeks, and more than 1.2 million within four days. It has since been viewed nearly 12 million times.

The best nonprofits use fun, too. Consider the number of charities that organize events in which walking, running, bicycling, and other competitive activities are used to encourage people to donate time and money. Virtually every major organization devoted to medical research sponsors such events. For example, Avon Foundation Walk for Breast Cancer events take place all over the country to enable local supporters of breast cancer research to participate. In 2008 alone, nearly twenty-four thousand participants raised more than $56 million for breast cancer research, and more than $265 million has been raised by the Avon Walks since the program was founded in 2003.[31]

Alex's Lemonade Stand Foundation gets it, perhaps because it was inspired by a child's idea. (Perhaps your foundation should invite a seven-year-old to its board meetings.) Adults and children alike enjoy building their stands—which can be as simple as colorful signs taped to foldout tables—as well as the personal interactions that naturally occur as people stop to quench their thirst.

There is strong evidence connecting personal happiness with being engaged and proactive in giving back to the world. Happy individuals are much more likely to participate in activities that are adaptive, both for them and the people around them.[32] For example, positive emotions lead people to produce more ideas and think more creatively and flexibly, which in turn encourage imagination and enhance social relationships. By making the volunteer experience fun for your supporters, you increase the probability that they will continue to give—and give more—of their time and money.

Another way to harness the power of fun is game play; it taps into our innate competitiveness and desire for recognition. Just as we are wired to understand stories, so too do we seem disposed to turn situations into games. Games give your support team additional reasons to act on behalf of your cause.

Consider Foursquare (www.foursquare.com), a mobile application that mixes social, locative, and gaming elements to encourage people to explore the cities in which they live. Its goal is to "make cities easier to use," and Foursquare motivates users to do so with points, leader boards, and badges. Players are rewarded for being adventuresome—exploring different parts of the city, or visiting multiple venues in one night—and are encouraged to use the app to "check in" wherever they go, automatically notifying their friends of their locations. Many Foursquare users hook their updates into the Twitter stream or their Facebook status updates, so even non-Foursquare friends know where they are and what they're up to.

Founder Dennis Crowley recognized the potential to motivate this passionate game-oriented user base to do social good. At the 2009 Web 2.0 Summit in San Francisco, Crowley announced that Foursquare and San Francisco's Bay Area Rapid

HopeLab's gDitty— Changing Kids' Behavior Through Fun

The beauty of social media is that they cross almost all demographics: age, race, socioeconomic status, location. HopeLab, a nonprofit organization working to improve the health of children, tweens, and teenagers who suffer from chronic illness, exploited that phenomenon as a tool in its campaign against childhood obesity. When HopeLab introduced its first hardware product, an "activity monitor" (gDitty), it devised a way to simultaneously reach two very different populations—children and their parents—and inspire them to take action.

The organization's goal was to motivate tweens to move more by allowing them to earn points (when gDitty is plugged into a computer, it pops up a website where participants redeem points for rewards, such as videos and gift certificates). But HopeLab also had to spur parents to act. Indeed, the parents needed to act first, as the gDitty device and its associated reward stream aren't free.

HopeLab created a three-pronged plan to mobilize these two very different groups to take action:

Create a social community among tweens. By allowing tweens to use the activity points they earn to create and customize their own sites within the gDitty online universe, HopeLab hopes to harness their passion for self-expression and bolster their self-esteem. Tweens can look at others' pages, see the activity data of other users, and learn how other gDitty participants have used their points to customize their online avatar and Web page. HopeLab is also experimenting with collaborative forms of social interaction to help promote activity. By creating a website that facilitates social comparison, social inspiration, competition, and cooperation, HopeLab intends to tap some basic human social motives to drive changes in individual health and behavior.

Use parents as "stealth" distributors. The activity monitor itself costs approximately $50. Few tweens have that kind of spare cash or, if they did, probably wouldn't spend it on this device. And although adults often won't buy preventive health services for themselves, they will gladly do so for their children. The parents need to buy it and then support its use—albeit not overtly, given the sometimes contrary nature of tweens. In that sense, gDitty operates as a fun, engaging "front" for parents' more serious devotion to their children's health.

Encourage parents to talk to each other and to medical professionals. A key marketing strategy for gDitty aims at making the product go viral through word of mouth among parents and their health care providers. Parents have been fairly well convinced by public health and media sources that obesity and inactivity threaten their children's health, but they often don't know how to get their kids to be more active. gDitty is targeted to parents as a simple solution to that challenging problem. The main marketing message: "It only costs $50, and it has been scientifically shown to get tweens moving." (In initial studies, the first-generation gDitty prototype increased high-intensity physical activity levels in tweens by more than 30 percent over the course of six weeks.)

Transit (BART) system would partner to encourage people to use mass transit, reducing carbon emissions from cars and improving traffic conditions. BART commuters received Foursquare BART badges and also became eligible for rewards, including free BART tickets. BART also listed tips for things to do near BART stations on its Foursquare profile page (www .foursquare.com/user/SFBART). The BART partnership is the first of what Crowley hopes will be many similar socially conscious partnerships around the country, encouraging volunteerism, use of public transit, and civic responsibility.

Groupon provides another interesting example. Founder Andrew Mason observed that local merchants were willing to offer deeply discounted goods or services if they could be assured a certain amount of demand. He developed Groupon as a social commerce service to aggregate consumer demand and secure unusual discounts through a collective action platform. The result creates value—and the program is fun and engaging.

Here's an example: a restaurant offers a $45 voucher for $20 cash if seventy-five or more people pledge to buy into the deal. Once the seventy-fifth person submits her information, the deal is on. Groupon's daily deal email receives over 7.7 million impressions. The restaurant owner gets both new customers and brand exposure. And the seventy-five (or more) voucher purchasers get a great deal.

Consumers learn the deal of the day through Facebook, Twitter, and email. To stand out and avoid the customer burnout that often accompanies frequent marketing messages, Groupon hired Chicago-area comedians to write copy. Groupon grabs attention by exposing people to great local deals on things they want. Shared incentives among potential buyers and their friends lead quickly to engagement. If someone likes a deal, she tweets about it, places it on her Facebook profile, and emails it to her friends. The friends have a chance to buy into something that their friend didn't just recommend but actually committed to buy. Those friends then subscribe to Groupon, tell their friends, and so on.

Groupon is the first to bring this level of online marketing sophistication to local merchants, most of whom, the company found, were unaware of how Facebook and Twitter could help them gain new customers. The fact that merchants only pay for Groupon when an offer reaches critical mass made many of them willing to try it.

In every city, there is one primary deal of the day and one side deal of the day. By 2010, Groupon was in almost 150 major cities and had sold nearly 8 million Groupons, saving consumers about $350 million.

Three Rules to Win with Game Play

Consider giving out symbols of status. Status symbols, such as badges, cost nothing yet provide players with a sense of satisfaction and achievement.

Display metrics. Twitter displays users' follow count, tweets, and links. For example, the Obama campaign's account awarded members points for introducing friends to the campaign, raising money, hosting events, and posting blogs.

Create leader boards. Leader boards are simple scoreboards that keep track of players' scores or accomplishments in a game. Such boards can list the names— or online user names—of the highest scorers, or they can be customized by players to reflect the scores of players they wish to track. Leader boards create further competition between players— most notably in single-person games in which players are competing against themselves to achieve ever-higher scores.

Design Principle 3: Tailor

One of the most effective ways to encourage people to contribute to your cause—and to continue contributing over time—is to make *idiosyncratic fits* between their talents, skills, or interests and what you need accomplished. The idea of idiosyncratic fits—opportunities for an individual to have unique comparative advantage over others in completing a particular task or goal—has been extensively explored in many business contexts. For example, people are more likely to join a loyalty program (such as an airline frequent flyer program) if they feel they have an advantage for gaining loyalty rewards over other participants in the program.[33]

JetBlue found that when a program is compelling enough, and naturally lends itself to sharing and some friendly competition, social platforms serve as an accelerant as customers Take Action. In 2009, a few months after creating its Twitter account with the reasonable goal of reaching its frequent fliers, JetBlue executives were surprised to find themselves with more than a million followers and twittering well beyond the "TrueBlues." They considered how to take advantage of an asset they never had before—real-time access to over a million people in a new social setting. They found their answer in October 2009 when they matched Twitter with their "All You Could Jet" promotion—one ticket ($599) that would allow customers to fly as many routes as they wanted within thirty days. Fueled by Twitter, the promotion was wildly successful: the allocated tickets sold out within forty-eight hours. (They had to shut down sales a week early.) Perhaps more interestingly, without any prompting from JetBlue, the people who purchased the passes set up a Twitter account and a hashtag, #AYCJ, so they could share where they went and what they did as they flew from place to place. A few people became local celebrities, attracting news media and being welcomed upon arrival as though they were rock stars. These events became their own stories. Further, these consumers (for example, @terminalman, who went to seventy-two locations; http://www.wired.com/autopia/tag/terminal-man/) started to connect with each other, tweeting

Engineering Virality

EXPERT INSIGHTS

By **Robert Scoble**, *blogger and coauthor of* Naked Conversations: How Blogs Are Changing the Way Businesses Talk with Customers

- **Don't get caught up in the tools; they're just tools.** Get caught up in the story. Make sure you think about your story, but then act quickly, learn, and iterate.

- **Focus on four (or forty) people.** ICQ went from forty people to 60,000-plus people in six weeks . . . and that was back in the 1990s. When you want your message spread, focus on the really active people—the connectors. Let them tell everyone. (Hint: the average mom speaks to five people a day; connectors speak to twenty to twenty-five people every day.)

- **Build networks inside a company.** Start with one person you know, and have him or her refer you to another, who will refer you to another, and so on. You can also use social media that way: start by getting in touch with a friend who happens to be one to three degrees of separation away from someone you would like to know, especially someone more "famous." This is more powerful than just going to that person directly.

- **Use social media to build your brand and cultivate the right culture.** Zappos is a great example; founder Tony Hsieh forces everyone to tweet, making them all "brand ambassadors." ComcastCares uses social media to help personalize the corporation as well as communicate a brand message.

with each other and becoming authentic embodiments of the JetBlue brand. JetBlue invited twelve of the most prolific twitterers to its annual leadership conference to talk about how this became its own culture, and how they individually used the experience.

To motivate people to act on behalf of your cause, then, you need to match their skills, talents, or interests with your needs. Whether being creative, as with designing new outfits in Gap's Born to Fit initiative; providing an endorsement or reference; or making a physical donation, as when people give blood because they have a needed blood type,[34] the more that people feel they have uniquely contributed, the happier and more satisfied they will be—and the more likely they are to spread the word or return to contribute more.

Design Principle 4: Be Open

It is imperative to prepare for openness, which means creating a platform others can add to, take from, and alter themselves. How do you create this necessary culture of sharing, and how do you build trust? One critical step is to design with the principle of sustained transparency. This is easier said than done. However, if you design for openness at the start, it becomes significantly easier to continue.

First, perceptions of transparency don't perfectly correlate with actual transparency. And indeed most companies believe they are far more transparent than consumers think they are. This gap between corporate perceptions and consumer perceptions is known as the *image-identity gap*. Psychological research shows a similar bias for individuals, who tend to feel that their underlying motives are much more open and transparent than others find them.[35]

The Importance of Being Open

By **Charlene Li**, coauthor of Groundswell, author of Open Leadership, founder of Altimeter Group

EXPERT INSIGHTS

- Embrace open leadership. Have the confidence and humility to give up the need to be in control, while inspiring commitment from people to accomplish goals.
- Start with one clear goal. Are you trying to create dialogue, provide support, or innovate?
- Remember that it's about the relationships, not the technologies. Create a culture of sharing and build trust.

A second critical step to being open is based on design thinking principles. That is, if you ideate, prototype, and test frequently, you will—by definition—be designing for feedback. Showing people that they're actually making a difference is arguably the most critical aspect of encouraging action. The closer you come to real time in providing feedback, the better. People want to know they're moving, however incrementally, toward their goal. Show them the results of their actions (however small) as quickly as possible to retain their interest and encourage them to go even further.

Everywun.com provides an interesting example. Everywun is a nonprofit organization that offers fun, cost-free ways for individuals to contribute to a broad range of causes. Volunteers might collect books to send to Africa, shelter stray dogs and cats, or plant trees. Everywun posts their work immediately on its website, so volunteers can see how their efforts are helping their chosen cause. Volunteers also receive virtual badges to put on their Everywun profile pages or personal websites, depicting the causes they've contributed to, as well as a real-time metric that shows the good they've accomplished, such as the CO_2 emissions mitigated because of the number of trees they've planted.

Showing concrete results is critical, because nothing breeds success like success. Within just eight months of inception, Everywun.com was able to announce that membership had passed the 10,000 mark; that the website was experiencing

---

DonorsChoose.org Gets Ahead with Citizen Philanthropy

DonorsChoose.org matches students in need with donors. Public school teachers from anywhere in the United States can submit a DonorsChoose.org request to fulfill a classroom need— whether it's as mundane as boxes of pencils or as ambitious as a trip to Washington, D.C., for an entire graduating class.

Potential donors log on to the site, browse among the many projects that need to be funded, and choose whatever appeals to them. They can donate as much or as little as they want; once a project is fully funded, the materials or services are presented to the school. Donors get to watch the incremental donations to their chosen causes mount in real time, and the names of the donors as well as the amounts are posted as donations come in. Donors can also write comments on a Facebook-like "wall" attached to the project page.

What is particularly addictive about DonorsChoose.org, however, is the immediate feedback you get when you make a donation. When the project is funded, all donors are emailed photos of the initiative, a thank-you letter from the teacher, and a cost report that shows how each dollar donated was spent. Anyone who gives more than $100 to a project gets handwritten thank-you letters from the students. The founders of DonorsChoose.org call this mixture of choice, transparency, and feedback "citizen philanthropy."

Four Design Principles to Enable Others to Take Action

EFTO

Easy. Make it easy for others to act. Prioritize your calls to action. Your campaign is more likely to succeed if people understand what you need and can take immediate action.

Fun. Consider game play, competition, humor, and rewards. Can you make people feel like kids again?

Tailored. People gravitate to programs in which they perceive they are uniquely advantaged to have disproportionate impact.

Open. No one should have to ask permission to act. Provide a frame—your POV (point of view) and a story—and empower others.

monthly page views of 540,000; that Twitter followers numbered 16,000; and that Everywun electronic badges posted online by volunteers numbered more than 5,000.

Being open and choosing the right metrics to enable feedback are the final design principles for wing 4 because your ability to execute them rests on successful implementation of the skills you've already learned in the previous wings. Furthermore, they bring together the entire framework. Specifically, the metrics you choose to measure your cause must link wing 4 (Take Action) to wing 1 (Think Focused). They should reflect your project's specific goal and dramatize how that goal is incrementally closer than before—as a result of individual contributions. If possible, place the current status of your project in a historical context. One effective strategy is to use a timeline that depicts progress at specific time intervals or important milestones.

Getting Started with Take Action

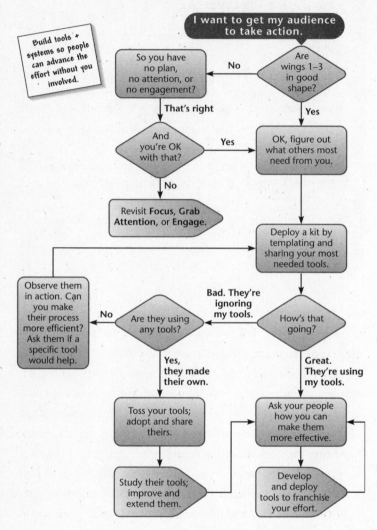

Feedback is motivating not only for users but for you: it provides the information you need to refine your effort and the energy you need to keep going.

In summary, ideate frequently, operate cheaply, and put in place online analytical tools to track performance. If people are unhappy, ask why, and acknowledge their feedback. If people are happy, ask why, and then make the campaign iterative with replicable tactics and usable templates. The fourth and final wing in the Dragonfly Model, Take Action, is the culmination of everything you've done to date to get others to support you in meeting your goals. By concentrating on the all-important "ask," using the strategies outlined in this chapter, you can successfully close the loop on your earlier successes: *focusing* your efforts, *grabbing attention,* and *engaging* users by spurring them to *take action.* With the right set-up, one small ask can garner great, perhaps world-changing results.

Onward and Upward

You're Flying! Now What?

Our hope is to provide a playbook that will empower you to bring about real change. People are often disillusioned by the idea of tackling a seemingly large social goal—it is easy to believe that you, as an individual, can't have any real impact. However, when you remember that you have the power to affect just one human, in one measurable way, the illusion of helplessness dissipates, and you feel inspired to make a difference.

Stanford Business School students are excellent examples of how one can make change with nothing but passion, a clear goal, and a YouTube login. In ten short weeks, they came together in groups of two and three to promote their chosen social good, using the principles of the Dragonfly Model to organize and execute their projects. The results were nothing short of extraordinary.

Project Baby Warmth: Embrace created an innovative, cost-effective insulated sleeping bag to save the lives of low-birth-weight babies in poor countries. The students marketed their product through a touching and emotional video about a young Indian girl named Ananya, and asked their viewers to "Help us save lives through the simple warmth of an embrace." They effectively connected the small act of making a $25 donation to the monumental act of making a difference in a child's life.

The Unnamed Company created an online forum for artisans from Libya to sell their one-of-a-kind furniture and artwork to women in the United States. Buyers know they are contributing to the livelihood of a woman abroad, providing her money to feed her family, send her children to school, or invest in her own business.

The Beautiful Things Project focused on a cause closer to home, with a simple but meaningful goal: to create real-world art projects that bring people together and get them to stop, take a breath, and create more beauty in the world. The students' video documents a community-decorated canvas set up in their school's courtyard, with testimonials drifting across the screen: "This is so much fun and so unexpected," says one student. "I can't tell you how enjoyable this is. To relax and enjoy and not consume it quickly." The video closes with the sentiment, "I love it. I've had so much fun. When is the next one?"[1]

Although we've all witnessed the power of the Internet and such Web 2.0 tools as Facebook, Twitter, and YouTube to connect us to others, it is only now becoming clear that we can harness these tools strategically and thoughtfully to bring about massive change and drive social good. Furthermore, the ideas and stories told in this book help redefine who can effect these types of changes. A revolutionary idea to bring about change doesn't need to come from a multimillion-dollar company or a well-designed nonprofit: it can come from you or someone like you armed with a detailed plan of action. "Never doubt that a small group of thoughtful committed citizens can change the world," Margaret Mead once said. "Indeed, it is the only thing that ever has."

Our work centers on the promotion of social good. The very phrase *social good* means different things to different people; we define it as a good or service that benefits the largest number of people in the greatest possible way (while minimizing the negative unintended consequences).

We want to rewrite the rules attached to social good. Although classic categories of social good center around education, environment, health, sustainability, community, and arts and culture, our definition is decidedly broader. We extend the scope of social good to include building trust, creating opportunity, improving self-esteem, and cultivating happiness. Why? Because the ability to motivate social good is increasing, particularly with the use of social technology. *The Dragonfly Effect* studies how design thinking—with its focus on deep empathy, hypothesis creation, and rapid prototyping and testing—can lead to an innovative perspective that fosters new ways of pursuing social good. It also demonstrates how our broader definition of social good better illuminates ways that social good aligns with profit goals. We know that doing good can be both fulfilling and profitable.

Dual Goals:
Cultivating Social Good and Profitability at the Same Time

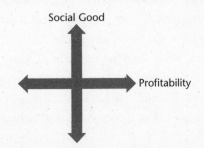

Social Good

Profitability

Research shows that a multiplier effect can result when social good is linked to profit-making endeavors. Many people currently labor under the delusion that creating good in the world can't align with making money. It's time to discard that false belief. Making a profit and creating social good are not opposite poles on one continuum. They are two independent dimensions—two goals that can and should coexist and be pursued together.[2] With this bigger-picture perspective, companies can better align their business models with their greater-good goals. Currently, most large companies have a "corporate social responsibility" arm that is disassociated (often completely) from the business model and the brand. However, when companies integrate social good goals into their business model (as eBay, Word of Good, Starbucks, Nike, salesforce.com, and Google have), they make more money and create more good.

John Mackey, CEO of Whole Foods, says, "Who says that 'making money' has to be the primary purpose or goal for businesses?" In fact, he argues that profits are highest when a business is driven by a higher purpose (for example, employee and customer satisfaction or the most sustainable products). To identify optimal business models, Mackey believes that we need to do a better job of looking for synergies, rather than trade-offs. Instead of seeing business as a zero-sum game (profits come at the cost of doing good in the world), Mackey suggests that radical collaboration and design thinking will enable us to find integrative solutions: "It will be the creative entrepreneurs that will solve the world's problems."[3]

When social good aligns with profit making, every stakeholder benefits. Since 1971, Klaus Schwab, the founder of the World Economic Forum, has been promoting the *stakeholder theory*, which argues that a company's top management must serve all stakeholders (the enterprise's owners and shareholders, customers, suppliers, collaborators, as well as the government and society, including the communities in which the company operates) to achieve long-term sustained growth and prosperity.

One way to think about this is how Jeff Clavier, founder and managing partner of SoftTech VC, frames it around passion. You can engineer a company for social good, he says, which can increase feelings of passion in all stakeholders. If you scale sustainable models (like TOMS Shoes is doing), that social good becomes self-perpetuating and infectious. Consider the ripple effect of reaching the people who share your passion.

All the people profiled in this book are people just like you and me—individuals with a goal, a passion, and a desire or need to get others involved. It is our hope that their stories show that you can elicit meaningful impact if you take your goal and funnel it into the right channels.

The Fear Factor

You've focused on a single goal, found a way to grab attention, determined how to personally engage your audience, and identified strategies to enable them to take action. You've invested a lot of thought, time, and energy. Only one dark question looms: Can this really work?

In his book *Fifth Mountain*, Paulo Coelho noted, "The fear of failure is worse than failure itself." Although speeding toward any goal might feel overwhelming at times, it's imperative that you don't get bogged down, but rather remain motivated and continue pursuing your goal. After all, you never know if that next email you send, that next Facebook group you create, or that next video you upload is going to be the one that reaches people in a meaningful way.

Studies suggest that risk aversion (both in people's lives and within organizations) stems from fear of failure. Fear of failure, or fear of losing the status quo, fosters inaction. In other words, fear is the enemy of change and innovation.

Here's the good news: it's possible to control your fear. Fear lies in the amygdala, the part of the brain associated with pain.[4] When you experience a problem with which you are not familiar, that activates the amygdala, which produces fearful responses. However, there are many simple ways to shift this reaction, tricking the amygdala to respond differently.

Samasource: Doing Well by Doing Good

Samasource is an organization that melds for-profit and non-profit forces and efforts, maximizing the power of social media. It enables marginalized people, from refugees in Kenya to women in rural Pakistan, to receive life-changing economic opportunities through "microwork"—small quantities of labor that can be done anytime and anywhere, usually via the Internet. Although Samasource pays only small sums for this work, it is enough to make a huge difference in the lives of women, young people, and refugees.

The Samasource workforce in turn helps socially conscious companies, nonprofits, and entrepreneurs buy services at reasonable prices. Samasource's business plan is based on three factors: (1) it chooses its "partners" (locally owned small businesses, nonprofits, and home-based workers) using strict criteria to ensure that they meet quality work standards; (2) it provides free business training to its partners to help them get started on their microwork businesses; and (3) it markets the services provided by its partners to paying clients in the United States.

Fostering a culture of rapid prototyping is one way. Most organizations and individuals struggle with experimentation and prototyping, refraining from introducing ideas or products until they consider them fully formed. But a design thinking culture encourages quick, cheap prototyping as part of the creative process, not just as a way of validating finished ideas. Don't get stalled by overthinking, overplanning, and overbrainstorming. Resist the temptation to always have a big plan before taking the next step.

Samasource: Applying the Dragonfly Model

Here are the keys to Samasource's success, in terms of the four wings of the Dragonfly Model:

- **Focus.** Help women, young people, and refugees in impoverished countries earn a viable living through dignified work.
- **Grab Attention.** Stress that the high unemployment rate and lack of hope in developing countries lead to the kind of disenfranchisement and anger that is a prime breeding ground for terrorism, gangs, and other social ills.
- **Engage.** Tell the stories of both the individuals who perform the work and the companies that employ them.
- **Take Action.** Offer three levels of action depending on the time and resources of donors. The top action is to give jobs to the Samasource workforce; the next level is to give money; the most basic level is to be a supporter who spreads the word about Samasource.

To date Samasource has worked with twenty-three small businesses, nonprofit training centers, and rural data centers on projects for more than seventy-five clients, to create dignified jobs for more than eight hundred marginalized individuals in Kenya, Uganda, Cameroon, Ghana, and Pakistan.

Another effective—and fun—way to overcome fear is to set up a reward system. Rewards have been linked to activation of the dopamine system—responsible for feelings of enjoyment, energy, passion, and motivation. We're not talking about big-ticket items; rewards are just as powerful if they are small and meaningful. And even the smallest act of kindness—making a quick $5 donation, or responding to that email from a nonprofit looking for volunteers—can result in a surge of dopamine. Further, receiving the reward matters less than you think; it is the *anticipation* of the reward that activates dopamine. Small, meaningful rewards not only keep you in the race but actually motivate you to pursue the subsequent legs with more vigor.[5]

Another important insight from psychological research is the idea of *emotional buffering,* which sheds light on the ways in which emotions can be regulated. Our emotions seem to come and go as they please, but in fact we actually hold considerable sway over them. We influence which emotions we have and how we experience them. Studies have shown that we have the ability to regulate our emotions, making us feel better about an experience—even a negative experience.[6]

How can you think about buffering your emotions? One line of research shows that you can reduce anxiety just by watching a funny video.[7] For example, in one study subjects were given a stressor: they were told there was the possibility they would have to give a public speech (something that makes people's hearts race and palms sweat).[8] Then the researchers removed the stressor by telling the subjects that they would not have to give that speech after all. Here is the interesting part: some of the subjects then watched a funny film of a puppy playing with his owner, others watched a film that was neutral, and still others watched one that was sad. The research marked the time it took for each subject to recover from the threat of the public speech. Those who watched the amusing video were much quicker to return to a resting state. So when your project gets challenging—as all projects do at some point—allow yourself the time to do something fun: enjoy a lemonade in the sun, watch a funny movie. You'll actually save time overall by reducing your stress more quickly.

Strategic Use of Expectations

A basic premise of the Dragonfly Model is that a single, concrete, measurable goal is necessary to serve as the engine— as well as a North Star and benchmark. However, for many people, that single goal might be too lofty, which can quickly lead to self-defeat and dejection. In Wing 1, we discussed the importance of thinking small and staying focused. Now, at the close of the process, we'd like to revisit the importance of realistic expectations. We're not talking about mustering up confidence or lowering the bar. We're talking about establishing a progression of practical, doable goals to help you achieve your greater goal.

As you work toward a goal, you might start to feel stress, as your goal seems out of reach or too broad. If that happens, if you close your laptop thinking, "I had these plans; I didn't meet them; I'm a failure [and nobody likes me]," then you go to bed feeling defeated. Even worse, the feeling of failure can affect your subsequent performance.[9]

This effect was demonstrated by researchers who found that students who set an ambitious deadline for a project ended up turning it in *much later* than those who had set an achievable deadline. Those overly ambitious students also performed worse than their peers. Researchers sum this up as "managing the delicate balance between desirability and feasibility aspects." But it is as simple as recognizing the dichotomy between stretch goals and realistic goals, and refocusing on the realistic aspects when the stretch goals become untenable or overwhelming.

Another way of looking at goals is to divide them into prevention- and promotion-based goals. We recruited hundreds of students and ran a series of experiments to test the power of both. One study involved a group of students facing midterms, who either perceived the exams as "soon, only a week away" or "still a full week away." These students were bombarded with sales pitches from a fictitious tutoring service: "Don't do poorly in any class!" (*prevention* goal) and "Ace every class!" (*promotion* goal). The students who perceived that the exams were bearing down on them usually settled for the prevention-framed service. Those who felt time was on their side tended to go for the promotion-framed service. Consumers tend to behave the same way. When shopping under pressure (perceived or otherwise), they respond to prevention-based slogans; if shopping in

Distinguishing Between Stretch and Realistic Goals

Think of **stretch goals** as "What do I have to do each day to achieve the aspirational goal?"

Think of **realistic goals** as "What do I need to do to not feel defeated when I go to bed?"

Always keep both of these goals in mind. You don't want to lose sight of the ultimate goal, but realistic expectations buffer you from burnout and allow you to stay the course.

a more relaxed mode, they gravitate toward retailers who lure them with ads that say "You desire the very best!" or "Our dealership has years of experience in meeting customers' dreams."[10]

How does this apply to the Dragonfly Model? The key is to be aware of the big, audacious macro goals, but success is more likely if you compartmentalize and shrink them into concrete, achievable micro gaols. Being realistic by staying focused on the more doable expectations, which correspond to the micro goals, will allow you to move more quickly and ultimately make a bigger contribution. You can't change the world overnight, but you *can* change the lives of individuals, one step at a time.

Overachievers Are Overrated

Not only is it imperative to set realistic expectations for the sake of your own mental health, it's a prerequisite to keeping your audience engaged. In consumer psychology research, there's something called the *perceptions-expectation gap*.[11] Consumers set expectations for a particular product or service at a certain level. If the product or service doesn't meet their expectations, they can experience disappointment, anxiety, fear—even anger. There's nothing worse than overpromising and underdelivering. If consumers perceive a wide gap between what you're offering and what you're providing, it can be virtually impossible to close that gap and regain their trust. To avoid that predicament, don't aim for perfection. Perfection is unachievable. Aim for what you can deliver by balancing a desirable goal with what's feasible. If you adopt a design thinking approach, this becomes easier because experimentation and rapid prototyping become the goal—not the unwieldy pursuit of developing the perfect solution. Team Sameer couldn't always focus on the twenty thousand names it needed to register in a few weeks; that would have been too overwhelming (and demotivating). There were plenty of moments when the most important goal was simply to make Sameer smile—something that was achievable and perhaps more critical in the long run.

Getting Ideas to Take Flight

Remember Volkswagen's Fun Theory and the video of the piano stairs that went with it? This clever campaign proved its thesis: things that are good for you can also be fun. It also yielded a successful media campaign. The video received 2 million views the week it debuted and has since garnered millions more.

What made it go viral? What makes anything go viral? Chip Heath, professor of organizational behavior at Stanford University, and one of his former Stanford GSB students and current coauthors, Jonah Berger, assistant professor of marketing at Wharton, study how products, ideas, and behaviors catch on and become popular, as well as what causes them to be abandoned. One common theme in their results: the power of emotion (and emotional connection) in making an idea spread.

In one study, Berger analyzed more than seventy-five hundred *New York Times* articles published over six months. The most frequently emailed stories in that period—the ones that went viral—were stories that evoked emotion. Articles that were mind opening, awe inspiring, practically useful, surprising, and positive were more likely to go viral.[12] Berger's research also illuminated the importance of word of mouth, which reinforces enthusiasm for products, and helps drive ongoing consumption. People must remain sufficiently enthusiastic about a

An Equation for Virality

(% people who pass on the story) x (% invitations accepted) x (average number of people invited) = ?

If the number is > 1, then the story becomes viral.

product to continue consuming it, but because enthusiasm for many products declines over time,[13] conversations with others can provide vital reinforcement.[14]

When working on your own goal, remember to capture emotion to draw in your audience, and then harness that emotion to spur the word-of-mouth phenomenon. This begins with targeting the right consumer, says Steve Knox, CEO of Tremor, an innovative word-of-mouth marketing service from Procter & Gamble. That consumer is not a trendsetter but a *trend spreader*. Knox estimates that 10 to 15 percent of U.S. consumers are trend spreaders. You need these people. These are the people who will tweet about your effort, leverage their Facebook networks, and call for action on their blogs. Speaking to these people early on amplifies your potential impact.

However, keep in mind the story of Sameer and Vinay. The people who spread the call to action were not necessarily trend spreaders or connectors—they were simply Sameer's and Vinay's friends and family members. Your connectors are not the same as another person's spreaders. Who cares most about your goal? Who shares your point of view? Your most effective influencers may not be the individuals with the most followers or fans; they may simply be your friends and family members whose passions and goals are most aligned with yours.

Making ideas spread also requires sending the right message. Knox contends that there's a marked difference between a message the consumer wants to hear and a message the consumer wants to share. When trying to get people involved in your cause, turn to your own best judgment: if you received this video or message in an email, would you send it along to your friends? Advertisers, marketers, and businesses constantly seek to quantify and explain what motivates a consumer. But we live in an era of social networks, when the power is not in the well-oiled plan of a marketer but in the recommendation of a *friend*. Making an emotional connection means connecting to other people, person to person, story to story, idea to idea.

The Dark Side of Social Technology

Throughout this book we've talked about the positive aspects of social good—saving lives, spurring medical research, building community—and the potency of the profit made by running something as seemingly benign as a lemonade stand. But what about when things go wrong? Consumers and employees have higher expectations when you focus on social good, and they're not afraid to voice their concerns, which on the Internet is kind of like using a megaphone that can be heard around the world.

Consider JPMorgan Chase & Company, which came under fire for the way it conducted a Facebook contest. One of the biggest online contests ever, the program was designed to award $5 million to charities chosen by anyone on Facebook. The bank promoted the effort as "a new way forward for giving," and the idea generated instant interest, attracting more than 12,000 users its first day and more than a million in a month.

Although the program was lauded for its generosity, ingenuity, and good intentions, as the contest unfolded it received criticism for its lack of transparency. The *New York Times* reported that at least three nonprofit groups—Students for Sensible Drug Policy, the Marijuana Policy Project, and Justice for All (an antiabortion group)—said they believed that Chase disqualified them over concerns about associating its name with their missions. They alleged that until Chase made changes to the contest, they appeared to be among the top one hundred leading charities in terms of votes, meaning they would receive $25,000, and possibly more, in funding. Three days before the contest ended, Chase stopped giving participants access to voting information, and did not make public the vote tallies of the winners.[15]

Chase responded that they removed the vote status "to build excitement," to ensure that all Facebook users would learn of the hundred finalists at the same time, and to give Chase the opportunity to notify the hundred finalists first.[16] The community didn't buy its story and considered the omission of the three formerly leading groups to be foul play. An open letter by Nathaniel Whittemore of Change.org lambasted Chase for "some pretty bonehead anti-transparency tendencies, which have hurt your brand with exactly the people you were supposed to be getting excited. Further, you've demonstrated a lack of understanding about how nonprofits really work. You've got an awesome opportunity to literally be the coolest contest there has ever been, but you've got some work to do."[17] Whittemore's condemnation reverberated around the Web through tweets and blogs.

There's another dark side to social technology: the appearance of activism where in fact there is inaction. Using social media to make someone aware of a cause is half the battle; getting him or her to take real action is the ultimate goal. And though the Internet has the capacity to engage a worldwide audience in social good, it also can breed apathy. Facebook groups like Save Darfur or Campaign for Cancer Awareness can amass hundreds of thousands of members, yet there are times when members of these groups, including the organizers themselves, fail to contribute in real ways to the cause.[18] Membership in an online group does not equal true commitment; it might even make people less likely to take action, because they feel that their online group membership lets them off the hook. In one study, researchers showed that when people talk about their intentions, they can be less likely to act on them because the talking gives them a "premature sense of completeness."[19]

Simply getting 100,000 people to join your Save Darfur Facebook group may not cut it. This is where your focus on a single, simple, important goal comes in. The final goal is not just to get 100,000 people into your group; rather, now that you have the attention of 100,000 members, your goals is to inspire and enable your group to take action. In moving forward, you must be cognizant of where the true power of social technology lies: not in the technology itself but in the people who use it. Movements that begin online must be backed by real-life action; otherwise, there is no point.[20]

The Power of Social Media

A year ago, if you were trying to spread your story and succeed at your goal, the process would have been much different (and much more challenging). And next year it will likely become even easier. (That said, don't wait until next year.) We're witnessing a rapid adoption of the social Web and benefiting from our ability to reach more people more quickly and more efficiently than ever before. Just think: Facebook went from a small dorm-room experiment to a worldwide forum with over 500 million users in just six years; in two years, Twitter grew from a service

---

The Greatest Opportunity Ever

By **MC Hammer**, entrepreneur, adviser, and cofounder of DanceJam

- **The gold rush is back.** This is the greatest opportunity ever to be an entrepreneur. Social media can be used to move and shake things without going through a bureaucratic process. Use social media to (1) keep your costs down, (2) tell your story, and (3) grab the analytics behind it and see what the people are saying. Smart is the new "gangsta."

- **Use momentum marketing.** Tools like YouTube, Twitter, and Facebook have lowered the bar of entry. The new bar of entry is how active you are. If you have a cool brand, you should think about being everywhere on social media. If you have the audience but no momentum, the perception will be that you're not in or hot.

- **The power has shifted.** It's a barbaric idea that ten people could have the power to decide whether your art is shown. Today, you don't have to rely on these people: post your art on YouTube and see if it gets a million views. Make sure you get ahead of a story by using social media before it becomes mainstream "breaking news." Let go of the old marketing mantra that told brands to mention only the good. Now we expect a disclosure of flaws—as you do with friends.

EXPERT INSIGHTS

that allowed small groups to share 140-character text messages with each other via SMS to a broadcasting platform reaching tens of millions of people. We are not living at the peak of this phenomenon. We're only at base camp, beginning our ascent.

"I would expect that next year, people will share twice as much information as they share this year, and [the year after that], they will be sharing twice as much as they did the year before," said Facebook founder Marc Zuckerberg at the 2008 Web 2.0 Summit. Saul Hansell of the *New York Times* quickly dubbed the prophesy "Zuckerberg's Law." It's too early to prove, but Zuckerberg's prediction has identified an exciting and powerful opportunity for spreading information.

To Go Far, Go Together

This book has described several extreme efforts to effect social change, most of them driven by pressure to move quickly: seven days to organize a protest, eleven weeks to find a bone marrow match, ten months to win the presidency. But the legacy of the Dragonfly Effect isn't about days or weeks or months. It's about the long term. To succeed in a sustainable way, we need to make a group effort. Al Gore, former vice president and master of the viral message, has said, "If you want to go quickly, go alone. If you want to go far, go together."

This quotation underscores a final important point: although this book tells many stories of companies and organizations harnessing social media to bring people together for good, Team Sameer and Team Vinay are its heart. The members of Team Sameer and Team Vinay relied on many strategies to get their message out, but what ultimately mobilized thousands of people was the personal, human touch the teams conveyed in every outreach. They used media to great effect, but their message was what counted most.

We've launched the Dragonfly Effect website (www.dragon flyeffect.com), where you'll find a community of people like you who are having remarkable impact by harnessing social media, sharing their ideas, stories, and resources. We offer how-to guides, templates, boot camps, and flowcharts. This community will expand with your participation, your ideas, and your drive to effect change. Coordination of efforts is key to the Dragonfly Model, where all four wings have to be in motion for you to get off the ground, gain speed, and take off. Small acts create big change, and working in concert maximizes your ability to go farther faster in any direction you choose.

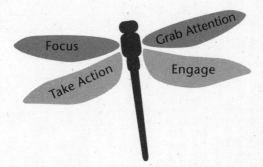

The Dragonfly Effect Model

	Wing 1: Think Focused	Wing 2: Grab Attention	Wing 3: Engage	Wing 4: Take Action
What is it?	Concentrate on a single outcome rather than "thinking big."	Get noticed by your target audience.	Get your target audience emotionally involved in your cause.	Spur your audience to actually act on behalf of your cause.
Ultimate goal	To concentrate all your resources and attention on achieving a single outcome	To get people to pay attention to you; and lay the foundation for *engaging* them	To "tee up" people to actually take action	To have your target audience volunteer time, money, or both to your cause
How do you do it?	• Set one goal. • Break it down into smaller, easily achievable subgoals. • Establish metrics to measure success. • Create an action plan. • Be specific and concrete. • Be true to yourself.	• Be original. • Keep it simple. • Make it grounded. • Use visual imagery.	• Understand what engages people. • Tell a story. • Mix media. • Make it personal.	• Make it easy. • Make it fun. • Promote "idiosyncratic fits" between contributors and requests for contributions. • Establish rapport with the target audience. • Provide immediate feedback in real time, reflecting individuals' contribution to your cause.
Reminder	One goal, one person	What is your headline?	What is your story?	What can someone do?

Getting Started with Social Media

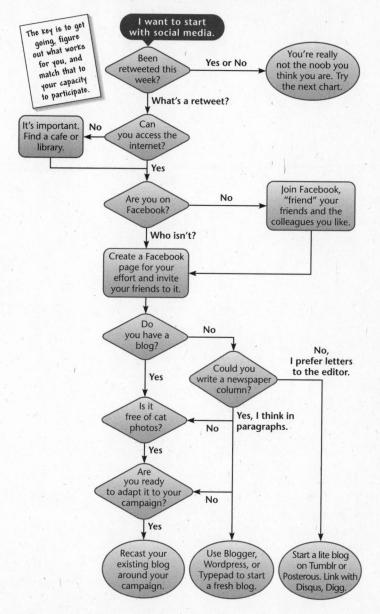

Afterword

Dan Ariely, author of
Predictably Irrational and
The Upside of Irrationality

The Dragonfly Effect, which you have just read, does an excellent job of showing how to accomplish something good, to help create a better world. If you've read either of my books, *Predictably Irrational* or *The Upside of Irrationality*, you know that I try to see things from a different perspective. I like to take things, turn them around, and see if they still work. In this same spirit, let's see what happens when I turn *The Dragonfly Effect* sideways . . .

Let's say I was a lobbyist for the U.S. banking industry. Far more than just my day job, this was my passion; the banking industry rewarded me handsomely, and I took on its power as my own. For my clients, I did everything I could to play the part of the puppet master with our fine men and women in Congress; I pulled strings and made deals as if I'd been born to do so. My purpose was to ensure that it remained difficult for regulators to figure out what my clients were really doing, which would allow them to keep charging high fees for banking services, and ensure that they remain unfettered and unharmed by regulations, limitations, and—most important of all—compensation caps.

I gave a lot of thought to how I could prevent, or at least meaningfully delay, any intervention into my lobby's affairs, and quickly realized it was going to be challenging. The banking crisis brought to the forefront a lot of financial

165

market activities that, until then, had been effectively obscured by mountains of documents, arcane language, and smart-sounding spokespeople. We had managed for years to keep ourselves below the public radar. But now that journalists and everyday people were asking questions about things they could never hope to understand and thus should never ask about, like derivatives and default swaps, it was getting harder and harder to hold to the status quo. What I sought was a return to the nice, cozy place where no one asked questions and so no one (technically) lied.

If only they would forget about us and go back to doing whatever ordinary people do, we could lie low and wait for the situation to cool off. What struck me in going through my machinations was that the public can be fierce but, thankfully, also has a very short attention span. All I needed was a distraction, something shiny and interesting enough to take people's attention away from my issues. But how could I make people care less about the newly conspicuous issue of banking regulation and divert their fury to something unimportant (to us, anyway) about which they could be equally passionate?

As fortune—mine and the bankers'—would have it, I had just finished reading *The Dragonfly Effect*. Here indeed were some powerful strategies. Using the principles of the Dragonfly Model, I would be able to create a movement that people could focus on and care about instead of banking reform. The issue needed to be visible and public; it needed to produce debate and inspire righteousness. I began thinking about earnest and passionate people, people who inspired and converted others to their cause. And then it came to me. Environmentalists. These days even an average Joe might look approvingly upon hybrid cars, disdaining those who run their errands in enormous

SUVs. I thought about Al Gore and his polar bears—a veritable symbol of the defenseless victim. Who wouldn't want to save something that adorable; who would care about overdraft fees if all the polar bears could swim and hunt to their hearts' content?

So I chose my diversionary cause: getting people to use reusable canvas bags for grocery shopping. It was perfect: reusable canvas bags are something that people see in use, they can create a discussion, and they can get people to look at others judgmentally in the supermarket. They can occupy legislators' time if their constituents inundate their phone lines and email boxes with comments about laws creating reusable bag credits and other such things. It would inspire them to fight for a definitive victory in the battle for reusable canvas bags rather than struggle for nebulous "increased oversight" over an industry they didn't understand well at all. So now I return to *The Dragonfly Effect* and the main lessons on how to start an effective social movement that would get people to focus on the reusable canvas bags issue.

Focus

Clear enough. What is my singular goal? Turning to *The Dragonfly Effect* principles, what do I want my audience to do? Simple: I want to create a new mass movement—complete with publicity and cries for legislation, the whole shebang—for reusable canvas bags.

My progress indicators will be several. First, I will track the issue's presence in the press—how many stories and segments went out in the written and televised media. Second, I will measure the actual use of canvas bags and then holler from the rooftops (in the form of frequent tweets, fan page posts, and e-blasts) about the low level of their usage. Finally, I will gauge the frequency with which proregulation Washington politicians grandstand in front of cameras on my real cause, measuring progress in terms of the decrease in banking news stories. I set a 180-day time horizon to project completion (enough time to avoid a reform bill).

Grab Attention

I need something to turn the heads of the public at large, especially people who phone in, comment, or blog about current issues (as that's how the news outlets decide what to write about). Through video clips placed on YouTube, I will create a connection between the distinctive sound that a paper or plastic grocery bag makes when it's shaken open and the collapse of the ecosystem for a [cute species to be named later]. A fast-cut YouTube video will alternate clips of bags being shaken out at grocery stores with stock footage of marching fascists and images of clearly painfully dead [cute animals]. Each clip will end with "Paper or plastic?" "No thanks, I'm not a [insert cute animal name here] killer; I choose canvas."

When people who have seen the video or heard the catchphrase later see and hear groceries being bagged, the association will be triggered, and they will be prompted to say something or shun the guilty bagger and customer.

Engage

How do I make people care enough to do what I want? Did I mention that the [cute animal] is dying because of your grocery bags? I will create a simple and picture-laden website with comments enabled, chronicling the story of the life and earnestness of the [cute animal] and how it mates for life and how much it cares for its young, while noting that the [cute animal] is dying because people don't care enough to use canvas bags.

I will set up a forum where experts discuss the ineffectiveness of merely recycling bags—arguably it demands more energy than it saves. I'll balance the negative with the positive to get people on board. The canvas bags we offer will be handmade by villagers in [poor country]. There will be pictures of them smiling broadly as they stitch them together; this bag program will not only help the environment but also provide a respectable source of income to the developing world.

Next, I will get friends of friends to pass a link to the story to a few young celebrities. Once this gets enough retweets and comments, we will bring this to the attention of the major and minor grocery chains, inquiring about the state of their reusable bag program, including but not limited to such questions as Do they have a program? How much do they charge for canvas bags? Isn't that too much to charge—shouldn't they provide them for free? Do they give people a discount for shopping with a canvas bag? What about a reusable bag credit—a few cents off the total for being so thoughtful? Oh really, why not? And so on.

The most important element of the distraction, though, is that switching to canvas bags is a difficult change to make, so this will require a sustained effort on the part of our crusaders. It's incredibly hard to remember to return the bag to the car after putting the groceries away, and to bring it from the car into the store. It's such a small thing, and seemingly so easy to fix, if only enough attention were paid. So people will care; they will be passionate about raising awareness of the issue, yet others will continuously fail, making it almost impossible to completely phase out the offending bags.

Take Action

How do I get people to take up my cause, as if it were their own? It's simple, really. I use the Twitter and YouTube platforms to stoke interest and point out that people need to do more than just use canvas bags themselves—they need to get everyone they know and see to do it too. I will incorporate a call to action targeted at people who do grocery shopping the most—caring parents—and encourage them to raise awareness among their friends and neighbors and put pressure on their local grocery chains and on public officials. I'll turn the nation's children into a youth army by convincing them through school programs that they too can help, if only they pester their parents enough. They'll look at their parents with sadness and shame whenever they use a disposable bag. And what parent wouldn't be affected by that?

Once I've gathered some people to the cause, I will create a package of tools that gives the motivated canvas bag acolyte all she needs to stage an awareness-building petition-signing presence at her local grocery store—a "grocery bag intervention in a box." The kit will include all one needs to know about where and how to legally set up a presence in front of a local grocery store; predesigned signs and petition forms; template text for emails to friends as well as for the local grocery store manager, the mayor, and the principals and superintendents of the local schools; and guidelines for using a Flip Video camera to capture and share the events on YouTube. I will create a

Facebook group to serve as the hub of social sharing activity, and will quickly appoint the first most concerned person to "coadminister" it with me. Finally, I will quietly and slowly back away and go back to my day job, while watching the reusable canvas bag wave continue to grow.

Of course, this was all hypothetical. In the real world, my hope, my real passion, is that we will begin paying serious attention to the banking industry, enough to bring it under control. But the problem of misallocating our care and attention and effort is real. Once you understand how to get people to care, you also realize that you have the power to influence what people do, how they spend their time, and how they spend their money—simultaneously influencing where they will pay *less* attention and time.

We often think that we understand social media, but what remains a mystery, and what we really need to understand, is what motivates the people behind the social network. *The Dragonfly Effect* is the playbook for using social media. It is up to you whether you use these principles and tools for good or evil, whether you use them to do some good or just to create more distraction. As the saying goes, with great power comes great responsibility. And social power is no different. In a world where a wedding video can reach 50 million views, we all have a much greater opportunity to have an impact than ever before. Let's make it a good one.

Notes

Introduction

1. Meehan, C. "Technology and Society: The Power of Social Technology at Stanford Business School." The Technological Citizen blog, posted Mar. 11, 2010. http://thetechnologicalcitizen.com/?p=2854.

2. Kamvar, S., and Harris, J. J. *We Feel Fine: An Almanac of Human Emotion.* New York: Scribner, 2009.

3. Kamvar, S., Mogilner, C., and Aaker, J. L. "The Meaning(s) of Happiness." Research Paper No. 2026, Stanford University Graduate School of Business, 2010.

   Aaker, J. L., Vohs, K., and Mogilner, C. "Non-Profits Are Seen as Warm and For-Profits as Competent: Firm Stereotypes Matter." *Journal of Consumer Research,* Forthcoming, August 2010.

4. Rudd, M., and Aaker, J. L. "Expanding Time: When and Why Consumers Experience Time as More Expansive Versus Constrained." Working paper, Stanford University Graduate School of Business, 2010.

   Csikszentmihalyi, M. *Flow: The Psychology of Optimal Experience.* New York: HarperCollins, 1990.

5. Hatfield, E., Cacioppo, J. T., and Rapson, R. L. "Emotional Contagion." *Current Directions in Psychological Science*, 1993, *2(3)*, 96–99.

   Lakin, J. L., and Chartrand, T. L. "Using Nonconscious Behavioral Mimicry to Create Affiliation and Rapport." *Psychological Science*, 2003, *14(4)*, 334–339.

   Barsade, S. G. "The Ripple Effect: Emotional Contagion and Its Influence on Group Behavior." *Administrative Science Quarterly*, 2002, *47(4)*, 644–675.

6. Zajonc, R. B., Adelmann, P. K., Murphy, S. T., and Niedenthal, P. M. "Convergence in the Physical Appearance of Spouses." *Motivation and Emotion*, 1987, *11(4)*, 335–346.

7. Sy, T., Cote, S., and Saavedra, R. "The Contagious Leader: Impact of the Leader's Mood on the Mood of Group Members, Group Affective Tone, and Group Process." *Journal of Applied Psychology*, 2005, *90(2)*, 295–305.

8. Neumann, R., and Strack, F. "Mood Contagion: The Automatic Transfer of Mood Between Persons." *Journal of Personality and Social Psychology*, 2000, *79(2)*, 211–223.

9. Fowler, J. H., and Christakis, N. A. "Dynamic Spread of Happiness in a Large Social Network: Longitudinal Analysis over 20 Years in the Framingham Heart Study." *British Medical Journal*, 2008, *337(a2338)*, 1–9.

10. Benioff, M. *Behind the Cloud.* San Francisco: Jossey-Bass, 2009, p. 168.

11. Diener, E., and Seligman, M. "Beyond Money: Toward an Economy of Well-Being." *Psychological Science in the Public Interest*, 2004, *5(1)*, 1–31.

12. Sheldon, K. M., and Kasser, T. "Pursuing Personal Goals: Skills Enable Progress but Not All Progress Is Beneficial." *Personality and Social Psychology Bulletin*, 1998, *24(12)*, 546–557.

13. Sheldon, K. M., Elliot, A. J., Kim, Y., and Kasser, T. "What Is Satisfying About Satisfying Events? Testing 10 Candidate Psychological Needs." *Journal of Personality and Social Psychology*, 2001, *80(2)*, 325–339.

14. Aknin, L., Norton, M., and Dunn, E. "From Wealth to Well-Being? Money Matters, but Less Than People Think." *Journal of Positive Psychology*, 2009, *4(6)*, 523–527.

15. Gilbert, D. T. *Stumbling on Happiness.* New York: Knopf, 2006.

Kasser, T., and Kanner, A. D. *Psychology and Consumer Culture: The Struggle for a Good Life in a Materialistic World.* Washington, D.C.: American Psychological Association, 2004.

Sheldon, K. M., and Lyubomirsky, S. "Is It Possible to Become Happier? (And If So, How?)." *Social and Personality Psychology Compass*, 2007, *1(1)*, 129–145.

16. Diener, E., and Biswas-Diener, R. "Will Money Increase Subjective Well-Being? A Literature Review and Guide to Needed Research." *Social Indicators Research,* 2002, *57(2),* 119–169.

    Frey, B. S., and Stutzer, A. *Happiness and Economics.* Princeton, N.J.: Princeton University Press, 2002.

    Van Boven, L. "To Do or to Have? That Is the Question." *Journal of Personality and Social Psychology,* 2003, *85(6),* 1193–1202.

    Kahneman, D., Krueger, A. B., and Schkade, D. A. "The Reliability of Subjective Well-Being Measures." Working Paper, Center for Economic Policy Studies, Department of Economics, Princeton University, 2007.

    Schwarz, N., and Stone, A. A. "Would You Be Happier If You Were Richer?" *Science,* 2006, *312(5782),* 1908–1910.

17. Dunn, E. W., Aknin, L., and Norton, M. I. "Spending Money on Others Promotes Happiness." *Science,* 2008, *319(5870),* 1687–1688.

18. Mogilner, C. "The Pursuit of Happiness: Time, Money, and Social Connection." *Psychological Science,* forthcoming.

19. Moll, J., Krueger, F., Zahn, R., Pardini, M., Oliveira-Souza, R., and Grafman, J. "Human Fronto-Mesolimbic Networks Guide Decisions About Charitable Donations." *Proceedings of the National Academy of Sciences of the United States of America,* 2006, *103(42),* 15623–15628.

20. Brown, T. *Change by Design: How Design Thinking Transforms Organizations and Inspires Innovation.* New York: Harper Business, 2009.

    IDEO. Human-Centered Design Toolkit, 2009. Available at http://www.ideo.com/work/featured/human-centered-design-toolkit.

    Brown, T., and Wyatt, J. "Design Thinking for Social Innovation." *Stanford Social Innovation Review,* Winter 2010. http://www.ssireview.org/articles/entry/design_thinking_for_social_innovation/.

The Dragonfly Body

1. This email is abbreviated; please find the full letter here: http://faculty-gsb.stanford.edu/aaker/pages/documents/UsingSocialMediatoSave Lives.pdf.

2. Help Vinay & Sameer blog, posted Aug. 30, 2007. www.helpsameer.org.

3. Help Vinay & Sameer blog, posted Aug. 25, 2007. www.helpsameer.org.

4. Aaker, J. L., and Chang, V. "Using Social Media to Save Lives: Help VinayAndSameer.org." Stanford GSB Case No. M319PP, 2009.

Wing 1: Focus

1. IDEO. Human Centered Design Toolkit, 2009. Available at http://www.ideo.com/work/featured/human-centered-design-toolkit.

2. Beckman, S., and Barry, M. "Innovation as a Learning Process: Embedding Design Thinking." *California Management Review,* 2007, *50(1),* 25–56.

3. Brown, T. "Design Thinking." *Harvard Business Review,* June 2008. Reprint available at http://www.ideo.com/images/uploads/news/pdfs/IDEO_HBR_Design_Thinking.pdf.

4. Ibid.

5. Meth Project Foundation. "Montana Meth Project." 2010. http://www.montanameth.org/index.php.

6. Oudsema, S., and Wedell, R. "Unselling Meth." *Stanford Social Innovation Review,* Summer 2007. http://www.ssireview.org/articles/entry/unselling_meth/.

7. Taylor, S. E., Pham, L. B., Rivkin, I. D., and Armor, D. A. "Harness the Imagination: Mental Simulation, Self-Regulation, and Coping." *American Psychologist,* 1998, *53(4),* 429–439.

8. Liberman, N., and Trope, Y. "The Role of Feasibility and Desirability Considerations in Near and Distant Future Decisions." *Journal of Personality and Social Psychology,* 1998, *75(1),* 5–18.

9. Fogg, B. J. "Creating Persuasive Technologies: An Eight-Step Design Process." *Proceedings of the 4th International Conference on Persuasive Technology.* New York: ACM, 2009.

10. Thaler, R. H., and Sustein, C. R. *Nudge: Improving Decisions About Health, Wealth, and Happiness.* New Haven, CT: Yale University Press, 2008.

11. Bandura, A., and Cervone, D. "Self-Evaluative and Self-Efficacy Mechanisms Governing the Motivational Effects of Goal Systems." *Journal of Personality and Social Psychology,* 1983, *45(5),* 1017–1028.

12. Latham, G. P., and Seijts, G. H. "The Effects of Proximal and Distal Goals on Performance on Moderately Complex Task." *Journal of Organizational Behavior,* 1999, *20(4),* 421–429.

13. Bandura, A., and Schunk, D. "Cultivating Competence, Self-Efficacy, and Intrinsic Interest Through Proximal Self-Motivation." *Journal of Personality and Social Psychology,* 1981, *41(3),* 586–598.

    Manderlink, G., and Harackiewicz, J. M. "Proximal Versus Distal Goal Setting and Intrinsic Motivation." *Journal of Personality and Social Psychology,* 1984, *47(4),* 918–928.

14. Ambady, N., and Rosenthal, R. "Half a Minute: Predicting Teacher Evaluations from Thin Slices of Nonverbal Behavior and Physical Attractiveness." *Journal of Personality and Social Psychology,* 1993, *64(3),* 431–441.

15. Thaler, R. H., and Sustein, C. R. *Nudge: Improving Decisions About Health, Wealth, and Happiness.* New Haven, CT: Yale University Press, 2008.

16. Madrian, B. C., and Shea, D. F. "The Power of Suggestion: Inertia in 401(k) Participation and Savings Behavior." *The Quarterly Journal of Economics,* 2001, *96(4),* 1149–1188.

17. Johnson, E., and Goldstein, D. "Do Defaults Save Lives?" *Science,* 2003, *302(5649),* 1338–1339.

    Bertrand, M., Mullainathan, S., and Shafir, E. "Behavioral Economics and Marketing in Aid of Decision Making Among the Poor." *Journal of Public Policy and Marketing,* 2006, *25(1),* 8–23.

18. Gollwitzer, P. M., and Brandstätter, V. "Implementation Intentions and Effective Goal Pursuit." *Journal of Personality and Social Psychology,* 1997, *73(1),* 902–912.

    Bandura, A., and Cervone, D. "Self-Evaluative and Self-Efficacy Mechanisms Governing the Motivational Effects of Goal Systems." *Journal of Personality and Social Psychology,* 1983, *45(5),* 1017–1028.

    Becker, L. J. "Joint Effect of Feedback and Goal Setting on Performance: A Field Study of Residential Energy Conservation." *Journal of Applied Psychology,* 1978, *63(4),* 428–433.

Erez, M. "Feedback: A Necessary Condition for the Goal-Setting Performance Relationship." *Journal of Applied Psychology,* 1977, *62(5),* 624–627.

19. Ariely, D., and Wertenbroch, K. "Procrastination, Deadlines, and Performance: Self-Control by Precommitment." *Psychological Science,* 2002, *13(3),* 219–224.

20. Gollwitzer, P. M., and Brandstätter, V. "Implementation Intentions and Effective Goal Pursuit." *Journal of Personality and Social Psychology,* 1997, *73(1),* 902–912.

21. Bandura, A., and Cervone, D. "Self-Evaluative and Self-Efficacy Mechanisms Governing the Motivational Effects of Goal Systems." *Journal of Personality and Social Psychology,* 1983, *45(5),* 1017–1028.

22. Ibid.

23. Ibid.

24. Koestner, R., Lekes, N., Powers, T., and Chicoine, E. "Attaining Personal Goals: Self-Concordance Plus Implementation Intentions Equals Success." *Journal of Personality and Social Psychology,* 2002, *83(1),* 231–244.

25. Ophir, E., Nass, C., and Wagner, A. D. "Cognitive Control in Media Multi-Taskers." *Proceedings of the National Academy of Sciences of the United States of America,* 2009, *106(37),* 15521–15522.

26. Mento, A. J., Steele, R. P., and Karren, R. J. "A Meta-Analytic Study of the Effects of Goal Setting on Task Performance." *Organizational Behavior and Human Decision,* 1987, *39(1),* 52–83.

    Loke, E. A., and Latham, G. P. "Work Motivation and Satisfaction: Light at the End of the Tunnel." *Psychological Science,* 1990, *1(4),* 240–246.

27. Lehrer, J. "Blame It on the Brain." *Wall Street Journal,* Dec. 26, 2009. http://online.wsj.com/article/SB10001424052748703478704574612052322122442.html.

28. Kanter, B. "What Is the Distinction Between Social Media for Charity and Social Good/Systemic Change?" Beth's Blog, posted Mar. 20, 2009. http://beth.typepad.com/beths_blog/2009/03/sxsw-social-media-for-social-good-bbq.html.

29. Koestner, R., Lekes, N., Powers, T. A., Chicoine, E. "Attaining Personal Goals: Self-Concordance Plus Implementation Intentions Equals Success." *Journal of Personality and Social Psychology,* 2002, *83(1),* 231–244.

30. Aaker, J. L., and Chang, V. "Obama and the Power of Social Media and Technology." Stanford GSB Case No. M321, 2009.

31. Edelman Research. "The Social Pulpit: Barack Obama's Social Media Toolkit." 2009.

32. Ibid.

33. McGirt, E. "How Chris Hughes Helped Launch Facebook and the Barack Obama Campaign." *Fast Company,* Mar. 17, 2009. http://www .fastcompany.com/magazine/134/boy-wonder.html.

34. Cherwenka, A. "Inside the Obama Campaign: Lessons Learned." Happywookie on the Web blog, posted Dec. 8, 2008. http://happy wookie.wordpress.com/2008/12/08/102/.

35. Edelman Research. "The Social Pulpit: Barack Obama's Social Media Toolkit." 2009.

36. Lefkow, C. "Obama Has Huge Lead over McCain—in Cyberspace." *Agence France Presse,* Oct. 5, 2008. http://www.thefreelibrary.com/ Obama+has+huge+lead+over+McCain+--+in+cyberspace-a01611661659.

37. "Dinner with Barack." http://my.barackobama.com/page/content/ dinner.

38. Covey, N. "2.9 Million Received Obama's VP Text Message." *NielsenMobile,* Aug. 25, 2008. http://www.siliconvalleywire.com/svw/ 2008/08/nielsen-29-million-received-obamas-vp-text-message.html.

39. Miller, C. C. "How Obama's Internet Campaign Changed Politics." Bits blog (*New York Times*), posted Nov. 7, 2008. http://bits.blogs.nytimes .com/2008/11/07/how-obamas-internet-campaign-changed-politics/.

40. Samuel, H. "Facebook Makeover for Nicolas Sarkozy, the Man." Telegraph blog, posted May 21, 2009. http://blogs.telegraph.co.uk/ news/henrysamuel/9860449/Facebook_makeover_for_Nicolas _Sarkozy_the_man/.

41. Vargas, J. A. "Obama Raised Half a Billion Online." *Washington Post,* Nov. 20, 2008. http://voices.washingtonpost.com/44/2008/11/20/ obama_raised_half_a_billion_on.html.

42. Cherwenka, A. "Inside the Obama Campaign: Lessons Learned." Happywookie on the Web blog, posted Dec. 8, 2008. http://happy wookie.wordpress.com/2008/12/08/102/.

43. Talbot, D. "White House 2.0." *Boston Globe,* Jan. 11, 2009.

44. Miller, C. C. "How Obama's Internet Campaign Changed Politics." Bits blog *(New York Times),* posted Nov. 7, 2008, http://bits.blogs .nytimes.com/2008/11/07/how-obamas-internet-campaign-changed -politics/.

45. Cherwenka, A. "Inside the Obama Campaign: Lessons Learned." Happywookie on the Web blog, posted Dec. 8, 2008. http://happy wookie.wordpress.com/2008/12/08/102/.

Wing 2: Grab Attention

1. Heath, C., and Heath, D. *Made to Stick: Why Some Ideas Survive and Others Die.* New York: Random House, 2007.

2. Gantz, J., Boyd, A., and Dowling, S. "Cutting the Clutter: Tackling Information Overload at the Source." IDC white paper, Mar. 2009.

3. Wegert, T. "When Consumers Love Advertising." *ClickZ Networks,* Apr. 2004. http://www.clickz.com/3343411.

4. "Global Advertising: Consumers Trust Real Friends and Virtual Strangers the Most." *Nielsenwire* blog, posted July 7, 2009. http://blog .nielsen.com/nielsenwire/consumer/global-advertising-consumers- trust-real-friends-and-virtual-strangers-the-most/.

5. Brown, P., and Davis, A. *Your Attention Please: How to Appeal to Today's Distracted, Disinterested, Disengaged, Disenchanted, and Busy Consumer.* Avon, Mass.: Adams Media, 2006.

6. Quelch, J. "How Starbucks' Growth Destroyed Brand Value." Harvard Business Review blog, posted July 2, 2008. http://blogs.hbr.org/ quelch/2008/07/how_starbucks_growth_destroyed.html.

7. Simmons, J. "Starbucks: Supreme Bean." *Brand Channel,* Nov. 21, 2005. http://www.brandchannel.com/features_profile.asp?pr_id=259.

8. "Starbucks Fans Buzzing About Fair Trade Blend." TransFair USA blog, posted Sept. 9, 2009. http://transfairusa.org/blog/?p=1170.

9. Starbucks. "Starbucks Brings Thought Leaders Together to Develop a Comprehensive Recyclable Cup Solution," 2009. http://www.starbucks .com/sharedplanet/news.aspx?story=cupSummit.

10. Mather, M. "Emotional Arousal and Memory Binding: An Object-Based Framework." *Perspectives on Psychological Science,* 2007, *2(1),* 33–52.

11. Mogilner, C., and Aaker, J. L. "The Time vs. Money Effect: Shifting Product Attitudes and Decisions Through Personal Connection." *Journal of Consumer Research,* 2009, *36(2),* 277–291.

12. The Mozilla Foundation was established in 2003 as a nonprofit corporation; the Mozilla Corporation was created in 2005 as a wholly owned subsidiary to support development and marketing of Mozilla products.

13. Otten, L. J., and Donchin, E. "Relationship Between P300 Amplitude and Subsequent Recall for Distinctive Events: Dependence on Type of Distinctiveness Attribute." *Psychophysiology,* 2000, *37(5),* 644–661.

14. Gallo, C. "Grab Your Audience Fast." *BusinessWeek,* Sept. 12, 2006. http://www.businessweek.com/smallbiz/content/sep2006/sb20060912_913600.htm.

15. Dobele, A., Lindgreen, A., Beverland, M., Vanhamme, J., Wijk, R. "Why Pass on Viral Messages? Because They Connect Emotionally." *Business Horizons,* 2007, *50(4),* 291–304.

16. Godin, S. "In Praise of the Purple Cow." *Fast Company,* Jan. 31, 2003. http://www.fastcompany.com/magazine/67/purplecow.html.

17. Ibid.

18. Rogier, D., Leslie, S., and Aaker, J. L. "Dispensing Happiness at Coke." Working paper, Stanford University Graduate School of Business, 2010.

19. Hamlin, S. *How to Talk So People Listen.* New York: HarperCollins, 2006.

20. Fiske, S. T., Cuddy, A.J.C., and Glick, P. "Universal Dimensions of Social Cognition: Warmth and Competence." *Trends in Cognitive Sciences,* 2007, *11(2),* 77–83.

21. Berry, D. S., and Zebrowitz-McArthur, L. "Some Components and Consequences of a Babyface." *Journal of Personality and Social Psychology,* 1995, *48(2),* 312–323.

22. Berry, D. S., and Wero, J. "Accuracy in Face Perception: A View from Ecological Psychology." *Journal of Personality,* 1993, *61(44),* 497–520.

23. Yang, S., and Raghubir, P. "Can Bottles Speak Volumes? The Effect of Package Shape on How Much to Buy." *Journal of Retailing*, 2006, *81(4)*, 269–282.

24. Arnould, E. J. "Toward a Broadened Theory of Preference Formation and the Diffusion of Innovations: Cases from Zinder Province, Niger Republic." *Journal of Consumer Research*, 1989, *16(2)*, 239–267.

25. Rock the Vote. "2008 Accomplishments." http://www.rockthevote .com/about/rock-the-vote-2008-program.

26. Peracchio, L. A., and Meyers-Levy, J. "Using Stylistic Properties of Ad Pictures to Communicate with Consumers." *Journal of Consumer Research*, 2005, *32(1)*, 29–40.

27. McQuarrie, E. F., and Phillips, B. J. "Beyond Visual Metaphor: A New Typology of Visual Rhetoric in Advertising." *Marketing Theory*, 2004, *4(1–2)*, 113–136.

28. Nelson, D. L. "Remembering Pictures and Words." In L. Cermak and F.I.M. Craik (eds.), *Levels of Processing in Human Memory*. Hillsdale, NJ: Erlbaum, 1979.

29. Brown, P. B., and Davis, A. *Your Attention Please: How to Appeal to Today's Distracted, Disinterested, Disengaged, Disenchanted, and Busy Customer*. Avon, MA: Adams Media, 2006.

30. Schmitt, B. H. "Experiential Marketing: How to Get Customers to Sense, Feel, Think, Act, Relate." *Free Press*, Aug. 16, 1999. http://www .exgroup.com/index.php?section=thought_leadership&page=exp_mktg _company_brands.

31. Krishna, A., Lwin, M. O., and Morrin, M. "Product Scent and Memory." *Journal of Consumer Research*, 2010, *37(1)*, 57–67.

32. Sridharan, D., Levitin, D. J., Chafe, C. H., Berger, J., and Menon, V. "Neural Dynamics of Event Segmentation in Music: Converging Evidence for Dissociable Ventral and Dorsal Networks." *Neuron*, 2007, *55(3)*, 521–532.

Wing 3: Engage

1. Chang, V., Jackley, J., and Aaker, J. "Kiva.org and Storytelling." Stanford GSB Case No. M325, 2010.

2. Edwards, J., and Wasserman, T. "The Myth of Engagement." *Brandweek,* 2007, *48(25),* S8–S12.

3. Shields, M. "The Evolution of Engagement: Traditional Media Giants Catch Web 2.0 Fever—Will It Cure What Ails Them?" *Mediaweek* (Special report), Sept. 10, 2007. http://www.brandweek.com/bw/esearch/article_display.jsp?vnu_content_id=1003637110&imw=Y.

4. Digitalmediawire. "Webcast: TVGuide.com—A Case Study," July 20, 2006. http://www.dmwmedia.com/news/2006/07/20/webcast-tvguide-com-a-case-study-july-25th-2006-at-3-00pm-edt.

5. Nelson, S. "@DellOutlet Surpasses $2 Million on Twitter." Direct2Dell blog, posted June 11, 2009. http://en.community.dell.com/dell-blogs/b/direct2dell/archive/2009/06/11/delloutlet-surpasses-2-million-on-twitter.aspx.

6. Menchaca, L. "Expanding Connections with Customers Through Social Media." Direct2Dell blog, posted Dec. 8, 2009. http://en.community.dell.com/dell-blogs/b/direct2dell/archive/2009/12/08/expanding-connections-with-customers-through-social-media.aspx.

7. "7th Fleet Hits Social Media Milestones." Navy.mil blog, posted Nov. 24, 2009. http://www.navy.mil/search/display.asp?story_id=49839.

8. Leslie, S., and Aaker, J. L. "eBay: From Green to Gold." Stanford University Graduate School of Business, 2010.

9. McKee, R. *Story: Substance, Structure, Style, and the Principles of Screenwriting.* New York: HarperCollins, 1997, p. 11.

10. Steele, A. *Writing Fiction: The Practical Guide from New York's Acclaimed Creative Writing School.* New York: Bloomsbury, 2003, p. 2.

11. Murray, S. L., and Holmes, J. G. "Seeing Virtues in Faults: Negativity and the Transformation of Interpersonal Narratives in Close Relationships." *Journal of Personality and Social Psychology,* 1993, *65(4),* 707–722.
    Murray, S. L., Holmes, J. G, and Griffin, D. W. "The Benefits of Positive Illusions: Idealization and the Construction of Satisfaction in Close Relationships." *Journal of Personality and Social Psychology,* 1996, *70(1),* 79–98.

12. Pink, D. *A Whole New Mind: Why Right Brainers Will Rule the Future.* New York: Riverhead Trade, 2006, p. 66.

13. "Storytelling That Moves People: A Conversation with Screenwriting Coach Robert McKee." *Harvard Business Review,* 2003, *81(6),* 51–55.

14. Aaker, J. L., and Chang, V. "Obama and the Power of Social Media and Technology." Stanford GSB Case No. M321, 2009.

15. Forster, E. M. *Aspects of the Novel.* New York: Harcourt Brace Jovanovich, 1927, p. 27.

16. Goodman, A. *Storytelling as Best Practice: How Stories Strengthen Your Organization, Engage Your Audience, and Advance Your Mission.* Los Angeles, L. A.: A. Goodman, 2003, p. 1.

17. McKee, R. *Story: Substance, Structure, Style, and the Principles of Screenwriting.* New York: HarperCollins, 1997, p. 11.

18. Goodman, A. "A Bank That Always Builds Interest," 2009. http://www.agoodmanonline.com/pdf/free_range_2009_04.pdf. For more ideas on storybanking, see ImPRESSive, "The Art of Story Banking," July 1999, http://www.familiesusa.org/assets/pdfs/ImPRESS_story_banking6de2.pdf.

19. Gladwell, M. *What the Dog Saw and Other Adventures.* New York: Little, Brown and Company, 2009, p. 15.

20. Hsieh, T. "How Twitter Can Make You a Better (and Happier) Person." Zappos CEO and COO blog, posted Jan. 25, 2009. http://blogs.zappos.com/blogs/ceo-and-coo-blog/2009/01/25/how-twitter-can-make-you-a-better-and-happier-person

21. Cialdini, R. "The Science of Persuasion." *Scientific American,* 2001, *284(Feb),* 76–81.

22. Lakin, J., Jefferis, V., Cheng, C. M., and Chartrand, T. "The Chameleon Effect as Social Glue: Evidence for the Evolutionary Significance of Nonconscious Mimicry." *Journal of Nonverbal Behavior,* 2003, *27(3),* 145–162.

23. Goldstein, N. J., Cialdini, R. B., and Griskevicius, V. "A Room with a Viewpoint: Using Social Norms to Motivate Environmental Conservation in Hotels." *Journal of Consumer Research,* 2008, *35(3),* 472–482.

24. Small, D. A., and Simonsohn, U. "Friends of Victims: Personal Experience and Prosocial Behavior." *Journal of Consumer Research,* 2008, *35(3),* 532–542.

25. Ibid.

26. Small, D. A., and Verrochi, N. M. "The Face of Need: Facial Emotion Expression on Charity Advertisements." *Journal of Marketing Research,* 2009, *46(6),* 777–787.

27. Newman, G., and Dhar, R. "The Impact of Authenticity on Consumer Preferences." Working paper, Yale School of Management, 2010.

28. Rogier, D., and Aaker, J. L. "The Psychology of Authenticity." Working paper, Stanford University Graduate School of Business, 2010.

29. "Questions for: Jessica Flannery." *Stanford GSB News,* 2007. http://www.gsb.stanford.edu/news/perspectives/2007/flannery_kiva.html.

30. Avery, R. "Changing the World from a Toronto Home, $25 at a Time." *Toronto Star,* July 27, 2008. http://www.thestar.com/news/ideas/article/468025.

Wing 4: Take Action

1. Alex's Lemonade Stand Foundation. "Childhood Cancer Facts." http://www.alexslemonade.org/resources/facts.

2. Leslie, S., and Aaker, J. "Alex's Lemonade Stand Foundation." Working paper, Stanford University Graduate School of Business, 2010.

3. Flynn, F. J., and Lake, V. "If You Need Help, Just Ask: Underestimating Compliance with Direct Requests for Help." *Journal of Personality and Social Psychology,* 2008, *95(1),* 128–143.

4. Humane Society of the United States. "IHOP ACTION ALERT: Tag Your Status Update," Sept. 17, 2009. http://www.Facebook.com/note.php?note_id=165904233661.

5. IHOP. "IHOP and Animal Welfare," Oct. 29, 2009. http://www.Facebook.com/topic.php?uid=10036618151&topic=14312.

6. Fogg, B. J. "The New Rules of Persuasion." Royal Society for the Encouragement of Arts, Manufactures and Commerce, 2009. http://www.thersa.org/mobile/fellowship/journal/archive/summer-2009/features/new-rules-of-persuasion.

7. Strahilevitz, M. "A Model Comparing the Value of Giving to Others to the Value of Having More for Oneself: Implications for Fundraisers Seeking to Maximize Donor Satisfaction." In D. M. Oppenheimer and C. Y. Olivia (eds.), *The Science of Giving: Experimental Approaches to the Study of Charity.* New York: Taylor and Francis, forthcoming.

8. Durik, A. M., and Harackiewicz, J. M. "Achievement Goals and Intrinsic Motivation: Coherence, Concordance, and Achievement Orientation." *Journal of Experimental Social Psychology,* 2003, *39(4),* 378–385.

9. Braiker, B. "Facebook-ing Philanthropy." *Newsweek,* Oct. 26, 2007. http://www.newsweek.com/id/62168.

10. Kanter, B. "What Is the Distinction Between Social Media for Charity and Social Good/Systemic Change?" Beth's Blog, posted Mar. 20, 2009. http://beth.typepad.com/beths_blog/2009/03/sxsw-social-media -for-social-good-bbq.html.

11. Leslie, S., and Aaker, J. L. (2010) "The Nike We Portal." Working paper, Stanford University Graduate School of Business, 2010.

12. Community Counselling Service. "A Current Overview of Philanthropy and the Economy," Mar. 13, 2009. http://www.givinginstitute.org/ resourcelibrary/pdfs/US_Phil_and_Economy_for_Web.pdf.

13. "Volunteering in America Research Highlights." Corporation for National and Community Service, July 2009. http://www.volunteeringinamerica. gov/assets/resources/VolunteeringInAmericaResearchHighlights.pdf.

14. Independent Sector. "Giving and Volunteering in the United States 2001: Key Findings," Nov. 2001. http://independentsector.org/uploads/ Resources/GV01keyfind.pdf.

15. Samoan, E., Mc Auliffe, E., and MacLachlan, M. "The Role of Celebrity in Endorsing Poverty Reduction Through International Aid." *International Journal of Nonprofit and Voluntary Sector Marketing,* 2009, *14(2),* 137–148.

16. Domino, T. M. "Toward an Integrated Communication Theory for Celebrity Endorsement in Fundraising." Master's thesis, School of Mass Communications, College of Arts and Science, University of South Florida, 2003.

17. "How to Work a Crowd by Alexis Bauer - Ep23." YouTube video, posted July 20, 2009. iGNiTe. http://www.youtube.com/watch?v= LLDJG-F-maQ.

18. Mogilner, C., and Aaker, J. L. "The Time vs. Money Effect: Shifting Product Attitudes and Decisions Through Personal Connection." *Journal of Consumer Research,* 2009, *36(2),* 277–291.

19. Liu, W., and Aaker, J. L. "The Happiness of Giving: The Time-Ask Effect." *Journal of Consumer Research,* 2008, *35(3),* 543–557.

20. Strahilevitz, M., and Myers, J. G. "Donations to Charity as Purchase Incentives: How Well They Work May Depend on What You Are Trying to Sell." *Journal of Consumer Research,* 1998, *24(4),* 434–446.

21. Mogilner, C., Kamvar, S., and Aaker, J. "The Shifting Meaning of Happiness." Working paper, Stanford University Graduate School of Business, 2010.

22. Tsai, J. L., Knutson, B., and Fung, H. H. "Cultural Variations in Affect Valuation." *Journal of Personality and Social Psychology,* 2006, *90(2),* 288–307.

    Tsai, J. L., Miao, F. F., and Seppala, E. "Good Feelings in Christianity and Buddhism: Religious Differences in Ideal Affect." *Personality and Social Psychology Bulletin,* 2007, *33(3),* 409–421.

23. Liu, W., and Aaker, J. L. "The Happiness of Giving: The Time-Ask Effect." *Journal of Consumer Research,* 2008, *35(3),* 543–557.

24. Vohs, K. D., Mead, N. L., and Goode, M. R. "The Psychological Consequences of Money." *Science,* 2006, *314(5802),* 1154–1156.

25. Yi, Y. "Direct and Indirect Approaches to Advertising Persuasion." *Journal of Business Research,* 1990, *20(4),* 279–291.

26. Flynn, F. J., and Lake, V. K. B. "If You Need Help, Just Ask." *Journal of Personality and Social Psychology,* 2008, *95(1),* 128–143.

27. Cialdini. "The Science of Persuasion." *Scientific American,* 2001, *284(2),* 76–81.

28. Ibid.

29. Fogg, B. J. "Creating Persuasive Technologies: An Eight-Step Design Process." In *Proceedings of the 4th International Conference on Persuasive Technology.* New York: ACM, 2009.

30. "Volkswagen Brings the Fun: Giant Piano Stairs and Other 'Fun Theory' Marketing." *Los Angeles Times,* Oct. 15, 2009. http://latimesblogs.latimes.com/money_co/2009/10/volkswagen-brings-the-fun-giant-piano-stairs-and-other-fun-theory-marketing.html.

31. Avon. "Avon Walk for Breast Cancer Announces 2009 Walk Schedule in Nine Cities Coast to Coast," 2009. http://info.avonfoundation.org/site/DocServer/2009_Avon_Walk_Launch_Press_Release.pdf?docID =8902.

32. Fredrickson, B. "The Broaden-and-Build Theory of Positive Emotions." *Philosophical Transactions: Biological Sciences,* 2004, *359(1449),* 1367–1378.

33. Kivetz, R., and Simonson, I. "The Idiosyncratic Fit Heuristic: Effort Advantage as a Determinant of Consumer Response to Loyalty Programs." *Journal of Marketing Research,* 2003, *40(4),* 454–467.

34. Chopra, P. "Valiant Cancer Fighters Galvanise Indian Americans." *Thaindian News,* Mar. 31, 2008. http://www.thaindian.com/newsportal/health/valiant-cancer-fighters-galvanise-indian-americans_10032968 .html.

35. Alicke, M. D. "Global Self-Evaluation as Determined by the Desirability and Controllability of Trait Adjectives." *Journal of Personality and Social Psychology,* 1985, *49(6),* 1621–1630.

Onward and Upward

1. Meehan, C. "Technology and Society: The Power of Social Technology at Stanford Business School." The Technological Citizen blog, posted Mar. 11, 2010. http://thetechnologicalcitizen.com/?p=2854.

2. Aaker, J. L., Vohs, K., and Mogilner, C. "Non-Profits Are Seen as Warm and For-Profits as Competent: Firm Stereotypes Matter," August, 2010.

3. John Mackey's talk at Stanford Graduate School of Business is available at http://www.powerofsocialtech.com/search?q=john+mackey, Feb. 2010.

4. Adolphs, R., Tranel, D., Damasio, H., and Damasio, A. R. "Fear and the Human Amygdala." *Journal of Neuroscience,* 1995, *15(9),* 5879–5891.

5. Wadhwa, M., Shiv, B., and Nowlis, S. M. "A Bite to Whet the Reward Appetite: Influence of Sampling on Reward-Seeking Behaviors." *Journal of Marketing Research,* 2008, *45(4),* 403–413.

6. Gross, J. "Antecedent- and Response-Focused Emotion Regulation: Divergent Consequences for Experience, Expression, and Physiology." *Journal of Personality and Social Psychology,* 1998, *74(1),* 224–237.

7. Lekandera, M., Fürst, C. J., Rotstein, S., Hursti, T. J., Fredrikson, M. "Immune Effects of Relaxation During Chemotherapy for Ovarian Cancer." *Psychotherapy and Psychosomatics*, 1997, *66(4)*, 185–191.

8. Frederickson, B. L., and Levenson, R. W. "Positive Emotions Speed Recovery from the Cardiovascular Sequelae of Negative Emotions." *Cognition and Emotions*, 1998, *12(2)*, 191–220.

9. Cheema, A., and Soman, D. "Malleable Mental Accounting: The Effect of Flexibility on the Justification of Attractive Spending and Consumption Decisions." *Journal of Consumer Psychology*, 2006, *16(1)*, 33–44.

10. Mogilner, C., Aaker, J. L., and Pennington, G. "Time Will Tell: The Distant Appeal of Promotion and Imminent Appeal of Prevention." *Journal of Consumer Research*, 2008, *34(5)*, 670–681.

11. Oliver, R. L. "A Cognitive Model of the Antecedent and Consequences of Satisfaction Decision." *Journal of Marketing Research*, 1980, *17(4)*, 460–469.

12. Berger, J., and Milkman, K. "Social Transmission and Viral Culture." Working paper, The Wharton School, University of Pennsylvania, 2009.

13. Wu, F., and Huberman, B. "Novelty and Collective Attention." In H. L. Swinney (ed.), *Proceedings of the National Academy of Sciences of the United States of America*. Austin: University of Texas, 2007, 104, 17599–17601.

14. Stephen, A., and Berger, J. "Creating Contagious: How Social Networks and Item Characteristics Combine to Spur Ongoing Consumption and Drive Social Epidemics." Working paper, The Wharton School, University of Pennsylvania, 2009.

15. Strom, S. "Charities Criticize Online Fund-Raising Contest by Chase." *New York Times*, Dec. 19, 2009. http://www.nytimes.com/2009/12/19/us/19charity.html?_r=1&partner=rss&emc=rss.

16. Ibid.

17. Whittemore, N. "An Open Letter to Chase About Their Big Charity Transparency Fail." Social Entrepreneurship blog (change.org), posted Dec. 19, 2009. http://socialentrepreneurship.change.org/blog/view/an_open_letter_to_chase_about_their_big_charity_transparency_fail.

18. Hart, K., and Greenwell, M. "To Nonprofits Seeking Cash, Facebook App Isn't So Green." *Washington Post,* Apr. 22, 2009. http://www.washingtonpost.com/wp-dyn/content/article/2009/04/21/AR2009042103786.html.

19. Gollwitzer, P., Sheeran, P., Michalski, V., and Seifert, A. "When Intentions Go Public: Does Social Reality Widen the Intention-Behavior Gap?" *Psychological Science,* 2009, *20(5),* 612–618.

20. Meehan, C. "Technology and Society: The Power of Social Technology at Stanford Business School." The Technological Citizen blog, posted Mar. 11, 2010. http://thetechnologicalcitizen.com/?p=2854.

The Dragonfly Ecosystem

I n this book, we talk a lot about the importance of working together: the need for all four wings of the dragonfly to move in concert, the results of uniting successful marketing strategies of profit and nonprofit organizations, and the value of sharing information and making something better by working collectively.

The Dragonfly Effect is a theory we've put into practice and experienced firsthand through the writing of this book, the product of a massively cooperative effort. A little Googling taught us that there are 316 species of dragonflies just in the United States. We had that many different specialists contribute to the ideas in this book. These are the people who helped us get our heads together first—and keep them together throughout the entire process. We've been fortunate enough to work with some of the brightest minds in marketing, psychology, design, storytelling, and technology, all of whom have shaped this book. We're grateful to the innovative leaders of companies who have shared their stories and inspired us. We were very fortunate to have our friend Dan Ariely introduce us to his friend and literary agent (and now ours), Jim Levine, at Levine Greenberg. Jim saw the potential for this book when it was just the spark of an idea. He understood and respected our vision, and helped us make that vision a book. We are grateful to the entire team at Jossey-Bass, especially Karen Murphy, a talented editor, for her keen insights and her deep commitment to keeping us classy, as well as Mark Karmendy, Erin Moore, and Michele Jones—three individuals with an eye for detail, even under pressure—and Erin Moy, Cynthia Shannon, and the always wonderful Gayle Mak for constant support and enthusiasm.

Chip Heath inspired Jennifer from across the hall at Stanford. In creating *Made to Stick,* he helped us see how a powerful idea, properly channeled, can create good across domains. It wasn't so much that he made it seem easy (which he kind of did) to create a powerful and useful business book; it was seeing how much resonance and impact those ideas had. Thank you, Chip, for helping us take the first step, and for the insight and guidance you've shared along the way.

We are grateful to count Dan Ariely and his family among our close friends. Over the years, we have benefited from Dan's generosity—sending us gifts by mail, on seemingly random occasions, never with a note attached. (For at least a year Andy thought it was a hiccup at Amazon that caused a chair-hammock to arrive one day. When Dan eventually inquired if we found our hammock as comfortable as he did—two and two equaled Dan). Thank you, Dan, for your advice and support and for showing us how fun behavioral economics and, by extension, any subject can be in the right hands. To Dan, the membrane between casual conversation and hypothesis testing is highly permeable.

Carlye Adler has been a gift to us. We don't know from whom. That's one of the things about ripple effects: you can't always determine the source of the ripple, but you are constantly thankful that the ripple occurred. From our first introductory meeting by phone, we knew we had found a wonderful writing partner to stitch our work together. Ultimately we found that she is both a knitter and a sewer, contributing to this work many stretches of whole cloth. Thank you, Carlye.

✂

Robert Chatwani: *The Dragonfly Effect* would not exist without you. Because of your deep commitment and love for your friends, the dragonfly first took flight. Thank you for writing the initial story about Sameer and Vinay, and for the difference you've made and continue to make. This book is for Sameer and Vinay, who embody and humanize the ripple effects documented in this book. Through their lives, they have touched and influenced the lives of countless others. Both live on in so many of us. Team Sameer and Team Vinay are the result of truly inspiring people who have taught us what is possible: Sameer's and Vinay's families, along with Alice Abrahamaniam, Sundeep Ahuja, Bharath Chakravarthy, Hema Chakravarthy, Partha Chakravarthy, Sonia Chakravarthy, Shital Chatwani, Paru Chaudhuri, Dayal Gaitonde, Meeta Gaitonde, Nelly Ganesan, Veer Gidwaney, Lakshmi Gopinath, Prakash Gopinath, Brady Kroupa, Shobha Madhav, Chandrika Madhavan, Harini Madhavan, Radhika Madhavan, Uma Madhavan, Nick Myers, Bhavna Patel, Kirti Patel, Samit Patel, Seema Patel, Preeti Patel, Amitha Prasad, Girija Radhakrishnan, Kavita Radhakrishnan, Priti Radhakrishnan, R. Radhakrishnan, Aditya Raghavendra, Rashmi Rao, Keyur Shah, Shilpa Shah, Melindah Sharma, Sohini Sengupta, Kristeen Singh, Sandeep Sood, Shilpa Sood Shah, Anu Sridhar, Mala Umapathy, Arjun Vasan, Ashwin Vasan, Kris Vasan, Nimmi Vasan, Roopa Vasan, Jeff Young, and many, many others. It's said that a man is judged by the company he keeps. By this measure alone, Sameer and Vinay were extraordinary, and extraordinarily blessed.

><

A staggering number of smart individuals have played a role in developing the ideas that have led to this book. First, we are grateful to the incredible Stanford GSB students whose projects inspired the Power of Social Technology (PoST) class. This class has been truly transformative for us; thank you for making it so. A special thanks to those who have contributed their time, insights, and stories to this effort: Thomas Rigo, Michael Ovadia, Ja-Ling Or, Danielle Burke, Raja Haddad, and David Rogier. These students, as well as those who participated in How to Tell a Story, Building Innovative Brands, and Power of Social Technology classes, were the ones we had in mind throughout the writing of the book. What you have been able to do in ten short weeks is incredible.

Thanks to our many advisers for sharing their knowledge, unwavering support, and time—we would not be here without you. First are the PoST teaching assistants (TAs)—immense thanks to Laura Jones, who is a design-meets-marketing expert extraordinaire, and to Enrique Allen, who is a wizard of design, video, and behavior change. And thanks to the efforts and support of the Center for Social Innovation, in particular Meredith Haase and Bernadette Clavier.

We are indebted to the many people in the field who have graciously, openly, and enthusiastically shared their stories—and inspired us in the process. These leaders include Ed Baker, founder and CEO of Demigo; Robert Chatwani, eBay, cofounder of World of Good; Jeff Clavier, founder and managing partner of SoftTech VC and seed stage investor;

Dan Greenberg, cofounder and CEO of sharethrough.com; MC Hammer, entertainer and entrepreneur; Jessica Jackley, cofounder of Kiva and ProFounder; Oren Jacob, CTO Pixar; Justine Jacob, independent filmmaker; Sep Kamvar, incredibly interesting person and coauthor of *We Feel Fine: An Almanac of Human Emotion*; Beth Kanter, blogger and author of *The Networked Nonprofit;* Avinash Kaushik, analytics evangelist at Google and author of *Web Analytics 2.0* and the blog Occam's Razor; Loic Le Meur, founder and CEO of Seesmic; Dave McClure, angel investor, entrepreneur, and blogger; Sarah Milstein, General Manager and co-chair of the Web 2.0 Expo, and coauthor of *The Twitter Book*; Robert Scoble, blogger and social technology guru; Matt Wyndowe and Randi Zuckerberg of Facebook; Pat Christen and Steve Cole of HopeLab; Steve Knox of Procter & Gamble; Geoff Moore, author of *Crossing the Chasm*; Genevieve Bell of Intel; and Gary Vaynerchuk, CEO of Winelibrary.TV and author of *Crush It!* Finally, thanks to Anthony Luckett, Lauren Gellman, J. D. Schramm, and Julio Vasconcellos; Ben Hess; and visual storytelling mentors Nancy Duarte, Tracy Barba, and Eric Albertson.

The strength of the Dragonfly Effect comes from the organizations and individuals who are making it happen. Thanks to the insiders who shared the behind-the-scenes secrets of how social media helped win the White House: Joe Rospars, Chris Hughes, Sam Graham-Felsen, Kate Allbright-Hannah, Scott Goodstein, Steve Grove, Randi Zuckerberg, Chloe Sladden, and Brittany Bohnet. In addition, thank you to Meg Garlinghouse for Yahoo!'s inspirational and effective You In? Purple Acts of Kindness campaign; Greg Baldwin, for the equally brilliant

VolunteerMatch; and Pat Christen and Steve Cole, for the inspirational HopeLab. Thank you to Bill Meehan for sage wisdom and sharp insight (always with a single eyebrow raised).

At Alex's Lemonade Stand Foundation, thank you Liz and Jay Scott, Gillian Kocher, Samuel Richards, and David Brownstein. Thanks also to Dan Jacobs of Everywun; Andy Dunn of Bonobos; Aron Guadet and Gita Pullapilly of the Way We Get By; Jenny Carroll; Leila Chirayath Janah of Samasource; Jacob Colker of the Extraordinaries; Paula Dunn of the U.S. Navy; Suneel Gupta of Groupon; Ziba Cranmer, Patrice Thramer, George Huff, and Jennifer Paulson at Nike; Priya Haji at eBay's World of Good; Ben Goldhirsh and Craig Shapiro at GOOD; Mark Surman of Mozilla; Bobbi Silten, Brittany Sikor, and Scott Key of the Gap; David Clark at JetBlue; A. J. Brustein at Coke; and Arun Rajan and Alfred Lin at Zappos.

From the outset, we wanted to create something beautiful. Not just an inspiring story or a useful road map, but a book that reflected the simplicity, beauty, and elegance of the inspiring people and organizations it profiled. A three-year study of more than forty Fortune 500 companies by the research firm Peer Insight found that companies focused on customer-experience design outperformed the S&P 500 by a ten-to-one margin from 2000 to 2005. We wanted the dragonfly to "outperform," and we found our best shot at doing that when we trusted the insights of the organizations we studied and embraced the crowd. We engaged 99designs.com to develop both the dragonfly identity and the visual language of the Dragonfly Model, and we partnered with Stanford design students of breathtaking intellectual horsepower and expressive talent. We thank Emily Ma, who brilliantly inspired many of the designs integrated in the book as well as in alternate dragonfly universes. Her work with Nina Khosla, a Stanford design student and brilliant thinker, and Joe Brown, an insightful revealer of all-important details in life, transformed the research that serves as the backbone of this book.

We are grateful to several talented writers who worked to develop many of the case studies included in this book. Three amazing Stanford case writers worked on cases and caselets for the PoST class, which serve as a teaching platform for the ideas in this book. The über-talented Alice LaPlante created caselets for the class, work that heavily informed each of the dragonfly wings with research. Victoria Chang originated the key stories about Obama, Kiva, and the campaigns for Sameer and Vinay. Sara Leslie developed the key stories about eBay, Coke, Zappos, JetBlue, and Nike, connecting and infusing each with research on happiness and meaning. Thank you to the Stanford GSB administration, who made Stanford case-writing magic happen. We thank Courtney Meehan for her sharp, insightful writing and her inspirational column (http://thetechnological citizen.com/). Much appreciation to Lisa Zuniga for helping us work around the clock when necessary (and to Stacy Crinks who made the swing shift work), and to Denice Gant, Mae O'Malley, and Sally Thornton, who brought us snacks, forced us to pause and observe small milestones, and made us laugh throughout the journey.

We also thank Michal Strahilevitz at the Marketing Department of the Golden Gate University Ageno School of Business, Kathleen Vohs at the Marketing Department of the University of Minnesota Carlson School of Management, and Aimee Drolet at UCLA's Anderson School for reviewing a very rough manuscript and giving us valuable feedback. Thanks to Toshi Akutsu, who told us his story of Table of Two; Chika Watanabe, for sharing the memorable COOKPAD story; and Matt Hunter and Liva Judic, who saw our tweets seeking more international stories to highlight and who responded with their insights, allowing this book to better reflect international movements.

A sincere thank you to Barbara McCarthy, Jennifer's left hand (and entire mind); Anna Dickstein, Heidy Kwon, and Bo Ah Kwon for research assistance; and Nick Hall, Cassie Mogilner, and Melanie Rudd for inspiring research on happiness.

Last, but far from least, we thank our family. Jennifer's parents, Dave and Kay Aaker, whose inspiration is boundless. Jan, Jolyn, Toby, and Tim—siblings providing unwavering support. Sami, Maile, Kailyn, Landon, Sarah Elizabeth, Tyler, Kacie, Brenna, and Elliott for inspiration, along with Team Foster for help in creating businesses that transform the lives of our kids. And to Robin and T. J. Smith (one of the original Mad Men): your spirits allow this book to be written. When we were first together, we read the manuscript of T. J.'s great American novel, *Return, Jonathan!* the semiautobiographical story, never published, of a World War II returnee's struggle to resume a normal life. We can say with confidence that by publishing this book, setting it free to help others, we are making Robin and T. J. smile.

Finally and most important, this book is dedicated to our children, Cooper and Devon, both eight, and Téa Sloane, four. In *The Dragonfly Effect* and in our research, we talk a lot about ripple effects—how one small, concrete, focused act (like the proverbial stone thrown into a pond) has a radiating effect that ripples across distance and over time. Throughout the process of writing this book, we've experienced firsthand the ripple effect in action. Specifically, we've experienced how one good move ignites more. How else can you explain our kids sacrificing Saturday morning cartoons to run a lemonade stand to make money to help eliminate childhood cancer? That effort then further shaped their own passions: Devon is focused on helping a twelve-year-old boy, Hussein, through Save the Children; Cooper is bent on working with Kiva to empower entrepreneurs in developing countries; and Téa Sloane is firmly aligned with the Make-a-Wish Foundation (in the absence of charities singly focused on making people princesses). At the risk of sounding absurdly optimistic (read: slightly Pollyannaish), we're taking all of this as a proof point of the book's ultimate theme: our lives simply feel more meaningful than before.

The Dragonfly in Flight—Alex's Lemonade Stand
(l to r: Cole Foster, Téa Sloane Smith, Jennifer Aaker, Cooper Smith,
Andy Smith, Devon Smith, John Foster, Sophie Foster)

Téa Sloane Grabs Attention with a Handwritten Sign

About the Authors

Jennifer Aaker

A social psychologist and marketer, Jennifer Aaker is the General Atlantic Professor of Marketing at Stanford University's Graduate School of Business. Her research spans time, money, and happiness. She focuses on questions such as *What actually makes people happy, as opposed to what they think makes them happy? How do small acts create significant change?* and *How can those effects be fueled by social media?* She is widely published in the leading scholarly journals in psychology and marketing, and her work has been featured in a variety of media including *The Economist, The New York Times, Wall Street Journal, Washington Post, BusinessWeek, Forbes, CBS MoneyWatch, NPR, Science, Inc.,* and *Cosmopolitan.*

A sought-after teacher in the field of marketing, Professor Aaker teaches in many of Stanford's Executive Education programs, as well as MBA electives including Building Innovative Brands, How to Tell a Story, and The Power of Social Technology. Recipient of the Distinguished Teaching Award, Citibank Best Teacher Award, George Robbins Best Teacher Award, and both the Spence and Fletcher Jones Faculty Scholar Awards, she has also taught at UC Berkeley, UCLA, and Columbia.

A homegrown Californian, Jennifer has studied at the Sorbonne, and counts winning a dance-off in the early 1980s among her most impressive accomplishments.

Andy Smith

An economist and tech marketer by training, Andy Smith is a principal of Vonavona Ventures, where he advises and bootstraps technical and social ventures with guidance in marketing, customer strategy, and operations. Over the past twenty years, he has served as an executive in the high tech industry leading teams at Dolby Labs, BIGWORDS, LiquidWit, Intel, Analysis Group, Polaroid, Integral Inc., and PriceWaterhouseCoopers.

As a guest lecturer at Stanford's Graduate School of Business, Andy speaks on social technology, engineering virality, and brand building, with a focus on applying technology to address real problems. He is a contributor to *GOOD Magazine,* where he writes on businesses that embrace and integrate a social mission. He has also spoken at World 50, Marketing Week, Intel, TechCore, and Interbrand, and is on the boards of 140 Proof, ProFounder, LIF Brands, Everywun, and One Family One Meal. Andy earned his MBA at UCLA's Anderson School and holds an economics degree from Pomona College.

A gardener, gadgeteer, and serious tech geek, Andy is the creator of "The No Cookie Diet" (which he's still on two years later). Once bumped from a flight that tragically crashed, he has since learned to accept travel mishaps, and most everything else, with equanimity.

Spouses and coauthors, Jennifer and Andy live in Lafayette, California, with their two little dudes and a princess.

Index

A